ADDICTED & CONVICTED

GREGORY MCPHEE

iUniverse, Inc.
Bloomington

ADDICTED AND CONVICTED

iUniverse books may be ordered through booksellers or by contacting:

iUniverse
1663 Liberty Drive
Bloomington, IN 47403
www.iuniverse.com
1-800-Authors (1-800-288-4677)

ISBN: 978-1-4620-1853-6 (sc)
ISBN: 978-1-4620-1854-3 (e)

Printed in the United States of America

iUniverse rev. date: 06/14/2011

TABLE OF CONTENTS

DEDICATION

This book of poems is dedicated especially to the Lord, my personal Saviour. I must admit that I am grateful for my last duration of my imprisonment and for my wretched life that has been spared. For this period I may express my renditions. During this incarceration I met a real friend, Jeff White, as he encouraged my faith.

I am also grateful to my pastor, Elder Mack Henderson. He inspires my faith and the strength to be humble. He was there for me when I was about to give up. Also, my sister, Donna Marie, inspired me to continue in my writing and dedication to help others that suffer as we do.

My wife, Teresa, stood by me all the many years of my corruption and addiction. To her I dedicate this also.

Also, I am proud to praise a real friend that also helped me to complete this book with pride. This is Rose Sieverding who resides at Humboldt, SD. She is a very special lady and has been there for me.

ACKNOWLEDGEMENT

Self,

I believe my poems are self explanatory, and I have experienced them as real life situations. Raised in and around alcoholism, I chose the irresponsible ways that led me to deviance. For me to be responsible was to be obedient to parents and authority. I can only blame myself for my misfortunes and tremendous suffering. To start drinking at the early age it allowed me to suppress my feelings and emotions. I could be anybody I desired, but unfortunately I chose a life of deviance that today I dearly regret.

I allowed my alcoholism to cause me a lot of unnecessary grief. At the age of eight, I was placed in a juvenile facility for petty theft, for being incorrigible, for missing school, and, yes, for drinking. Looking back I expressed a lot of anger and blame; and, since that time, I've been incarcerated most of my life in foster homes, boys' homes, group homes, juvenile halls, and jails. At the age of 14, I was placed in a reformatory where my escape failed. That's where my resentments began and were practiced.

I've been through a few reformatories and then the penitentiary a couple of times. I was released just long enough to drown my sorrows in booze or drugs. I have moved to different places after failures and arrests: several fictitious Ids and 22 drinking convictions. I have completed programs in 11 inpatient alcohol treatment centers and five outpatient treatment centers all just to satisfy someone else or to win my freedom. Obviously that didn't stop me as my conniving ways cost me my second prison sentence which I completed in 1992.

Needless to say, my last grade of school was in 5th grade which I failed. I was also expelled from kindergarten. Serving a lot of time, I have educated myself without ever taking a true personal inventory of my attitude and all the excuses that I can come up with. I am now 58 years old and just recently have found my spiritual self. It took a lot of suffering before I was able to admit my alcoholism. My third wife, Teresa, has seen me through a lot of detox centers, jails, devious behaviors, and hospitals. She now stands by me as she sees the spiritual side of me. My convictions of my addiction saved not only this marriage but also of most importance, it allowed me to save myself. Today I feel as if I was rescued instead of arrested. As my favorite hymn says in "Amazing Grace", He saved a wretch like me. For that I am grateful. I have actually experienced my death at about age 26 from an overdose of heroin, secanol, and alcohol. I've suffered from strokes, jaundice, and hepatitis C. I had many chances; and as I look back, I ask Him, "Why me, Lord?"

Today I am responsible to choose and decide for my higher power, God, gave me that will. I have been baptized in my Pentecostal Church in Sioux Falls, SD. I have found my spiritual self within me. It took me 48 years to get honest with myself and do my best to be obedient to our Lord's will. With that I live with a positive attitude that has changed my behavior and I now have confidence in myself. Most of all, I am a spiritual person with a lot of faith and am a person who gets stronger every day. I'm not perfect and I will make mistakes, but with prayer and honesty I can correct them.

Now, it is my responsibility to share my faith, strength, and gratitude in these few poems with you. Concluding, there is a way if there is a will. It's your decision. We can suffer or we can rejoice.

INTRODUCTION

DEAR READER,

THIS LETTER IS TO INTRODUCE TO YOU GREG MCPHEE AND TO GIVE YOU AS LITTLE INSIGHT INTO THE MAN BEHIND THE WORDS. WHAT YOU ARE HOLDING IN YOUR HANDS IS ONE MAN'S DREAM, INSPIRED BY A DESIRE TO, IN SOME WAY, BE ABLE TO SPARE A HUMAN LIFE FROM FALLING INTO THE SELF-IMPOSED SNARES OF THIS WORLD. GREG HAS BEEN SURROUNDED IN HIS WHOLE LIFE BY ALCOHOL AND DRUGS AND THE RELATED HORRORS OF THAT LIFE TO LOSING TWO WIVES, JOBS, AND THE RELATIONSHIP OF HIS SON AND "GAINING" ONLY REFORMATORIES, POVERTY, PRISONS, AND A LIFE OF MOSTLY MISERY AND SORROWS. GREG WILL ALWAYS BE THE FIRST ONE TO ADMIT THAT HE EARNED AND DESERVED THE RESULTS OF THE LIFE HE CHOSE, BUT YOU WILL NEVER HEAR GREG SPEAK OF HIS EXPERIENCES WITH FOND MEMORIES.

GREG GREW UP AMIDST THE TURMOIL AND PAIN THAT ACCOMPANIES THE ABUSE OF DRUGS AND ALCOHOL. GREG, OF COURSE, DEFIED ANY HELP OFFERED WHICH FINALLY LEAD GREG TO GIVE UP HIS STRUGGLE ONLY TO FIND HIS REAL LIFE IN JESUS WHO CARRIES ALL OF OUR BURDENS. GREG'S NEW LIFE NOW INCLUDES A LOVING AND SUPPORTIVE WIFE, A RELATIONSHIP WITH HIS SON, THE BEGINNING OF NEW CHRIST-CENTERED FRIENDS, AND THE DESIRE TO WITNESS TO THE TRUTH ABOUT ALCOHOL AND DRUG ABUSE.

THE ONLY WAY GREG CAN ACCOMPLISH THIS TASK RIGHT NOW IS TO HAVE YOU SHARE THE CONTENTS OF THIS BOOK WITH SOMEONE IN NEED OR NEEDS TO BE ENCOURAGED. JUST LEAVE THEM A COPY TO READ AS THEY WILL SEE MORE HEREIN WRITTEN THAN ANY OF US ON THE OUTSIDE POSSIBLY COULD. THEY MAY RECOGNIZE

THEIR TERROR AND LONELINESS AND OPEN THEIR SOULS
TO OUR BURDEN-CARRYING SAVIOR.

LIFE BY THE BELL

Work Days

Wake up	6:00 a.m.
Breakfast	6:30 a.m.
Count	7:00 a.m
Work/School	7:30 a.m
Rec. Ring Out	9:00 a.m
Rec. Ring In	10:00 a.m
Lunch/Prison Industries	10:30 a.m
Lunch/Mainline	11:20 a.m
Count	12:00 a.m
Work Ring Out/Mainline	12:30 p.m
Rec. Ring Out	1:00 p.m
Rec. Ring In	2:20 p.m
Count	3:45 p.m
Showers	4:00 p.m.
Supper	4:30 p.m.
Rec. Ring Out	5:30 p.m.
Rec. Showers	6:45 p.m.
1st Period Rec. Ring Up	7:00 p.m.
2nd Period Rec. Showers	8:00 p.m.
2nd Period Rec. Ring Up	8:15 p.m.
Count	9:00 p.m

GREG McPHEE

SOUTH DAKOTA
PENITENTIARY
25478

Holidays & Weekends

Pipe Ceremony (Saturday)	7:15 a.m.
Catholic Church (Saturday)	8:45 a.m.
Protestant Church (Sunday)	8:15 a.m.
Brunch	10:30 a.m.
Visits 1st Period	10:30 a.m.
Rec. 1st Period	11:30 a.m.
Showers 1st Period	1:00 p.m.
Rec. Ring In	1:15 p.m.
2nd Period Rec.	1:15 p.m.
1st Period Visit Ends	1:15 p.m.
Visits 2nd Period	1:30 p.m.
Showers	3:20 p.m.
Rec. Ring In	3:45 p.m.
2nd Period Visit End	3:45 p.m.
Count	4:00 p.m.
Dinner	4:30 p.m.
Count	5:30 p.m.

INSIDE LOOKING OUT

TRUSTEE "COTTAGE" SOUTH DAKOTA STATE PEN.

PRISON FARM

NICOTINE VS. ALCOHOL

LIGHT ME UP AND SMOKE ME WELL;
AS YOU USE AND CRAVE THE ALCOHOL,
WE'LL PROMISE YOU'LL BE TORMENTED
FOR YOU'RE DETERMINED FOR HELL.
DRINK AND ABUSE VS. WELL.
FOR WE PROMISE YOU OUR POISON WILL TAKE YOU HERE
TO HELL. CRAVE, RANT, AND RAVE BEFORE YOU LAY IN
YOUR GRAVE.
WE CANNOT BRING YOU BACK AS YOU MADE YOUR OWN
DECISION.
YOU KNEW OF US BEFORE YOU WENT TO PRISON.
CONSUME US AS WE'RE ALWAYS FOR SALE.
WE'LL WALK YOU THROUGH THE PRISON AND INTRODUCE
YOU TO THE JAIL. WE'LL WANT TO KEEP YOU FROM THAT
PRISON AND THAT FILTHLY JAIL.
WE STAND TOGETHER AS YOU ABUSE US.
WE'RE DETERMINED TO TORMENT YOU THROUGHOUT
YOUR SHORT LIFE. PAY OUR PRICE AS YOU LIVE WITH
CONTINUOUS POOR HEALTH AND STRIFE.   YOU WILL
POISON US THOUGH WE NOT KNOW WHO IS FIRST.
YOU DECIDE AS YOU ARE BEING CURSED.
AT TIMES YOU DESIRE TO PUT US DOWN;
ONCE ADDICTED, YOU'LL ALWAYS TOIL WITH A SADLY
FROWN.
SO, DANCE WITH US AND SMOKE AS YOU DRINK
EVERYDAY;
IT'S YOUR PREFERENCE AS YOU USE US WHEN YOU PLAY.
REMEMBER OUR NAME AS WE PROMISE YOU A REMORSEFUL
GAME. YOU'VE HEARD OUR WARNING AS YOU ABUSE US.
AND, ALL KNOWS YOU'LL NEVER BE THE SAME.
KEEP USING US AS WE'LL PLACE YOU IN THE GROUND WITH
SHAME. THAT'S NICOTINE AND ALCOHOL -- SMOKE AND
DRINK US WELL.
FOR YOU MUST KNOW WE'LL PROPOSE YOU TO HELL!
THIS IS OUR WARNING --
        BLAME NICOTINE OR ALCOHOL AS YOU SMOKE.

AND, LORD, DON'T LET NICOTINE AND ALCOHOL BRING
THEM TO HELL. WE ARE EASY AS YOU MAY CRAVE;
ONCE YOU'RE ADDICTED, WE CAN'T PULL THEM FROM
THEIR GRAVE. WE'RE NICOTINE AND ALCOHOL;
ALTHOUGH WE CARE, WE MAY POISON YOU AS YOU SHOULD
KNOW.
WE POISON THEM TO TAKE THEIR HEALTH BEFORE THEY
WAKE AND CONSUME US NO MORE.

HEP - "C"

FINGER PRINTS

MY FINGER PRINTS WERE EVERYWHERE.
WITHOUT HESITATION TOUCHING PEOPLE WITH UNFAITHFUL VINDICATION.
I'VE BEEN LOST IN CONFLICTION,
RAISED IN CONFUSION, AND WITH AN ADDICTION.
I'VE BEEN LOST IN A NEGATIVE DIRECTION
WITH A FALSE SENSE OF AFFECTION.
I'VE BEEN LOST IN CONVERSATION,
BEING WITHOUT FAITH, AND POSITIVE REPRESENTATION.
I'VE BEEN LOST WITH AGITATION,
EXPRESSING HATE, AND AGGRAVATION.
I'VE BEEN LOST WITH ANTICIPATION,
BUT ALWAYS CONTEMPLATING ON MY REVELATION.
I'VE BEEN LOST WITH MY FINGER PRINTS IN A TRIAL OF TRIBULATION
UNAWARE OF MY YEARNINGS FOR MY SUPPLICATION.
MY FINGER PRINTS PRESSED ILLITERATELY THROUGH THE BIBLE;
WITHOUT THE WISDOM I ALLOWED THE AUTHORITY TO PLAY THE IDOL.
YES, I'VE BEEN LOST BUT NOW I HAVE FOUND.
THE FINGER PRINTS OF JESUS NOW GAVE ME A PURPOSE TO SPREAD THEM AROUND. BEING BLESSED WITH KNOWLEDGE AND PEACE,
MY FINGER PRINTS NOW HAVE WISDOM, FAITH, AND WILL INCREASE.
ALL THIS TIME JESUS INTENDED FOR HIS FINGER PRINTS TO BE WITHIN MY SOUL;
NOW THAT HE TOUCHED ME, AND I ACCEPTED, MINE IS NOW ON HIS SCROLL.
I'VE BEEN LOST IN A WORLD OF REGRETS;
WITH HIS PROMISE HE WILL ERASE MY DECEITFUL DEBTS.
THERE ARE MANY FINGER PRINTS UNDER OUR SUN;
WITH THE GRACE OF JESUS, I AM A GRATEFUL ONE.

THANK YOU, JESUS, FOR YOUR FINGER PRINTS OF SALVATION;
AND, THANK YOU FOR TOUCHING ME WITHOUT ANY HESITATION.

THE ALCOHOLIC FLY

THE FLY IS WORST THAN I;
IT GETS IN YOUR BEER AND KNOWS NOT WHY.
JUST AS I SMELL THAT TASTE, THE FLY AGGREVATES ME
AS IT IS FILTHY AND CAUSES WAIST.
THAT CURIOUS FLY --
IF IT DRINKS IN MY BEER, IT WILL SURELY DIE.
THAT IS THE ALCOHOLIC FLY.

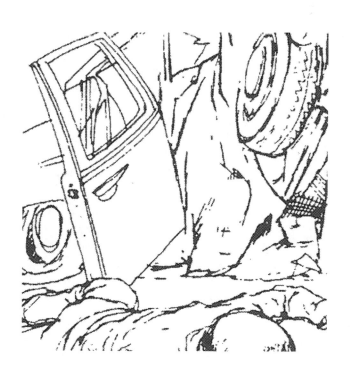

WARNING FROM ALCOHOL

BEHOLD MY FRIENDS, I, WHO AM ALCOHOL.
KNOWN TO MOST AS THE DESTROYER OF ALL.
SURGICALLY PURPOSED I WAS MEANT TO HELP THE MEDICAL FIELD.
THE GOVERNMENT PUT A TAX ON ME AND SOLD ME WITHOUT A SHIELD.
LIKE MOST, I CAME TO THIS COUNTRY WITHOUT A PASSPORT.
EVER SINCE THEN I'VE BEEN CURSED AND SOUGHT,
CAUSING PEOPLE TO STEAL, SO I COULD BE BOUGHT.

IN ITALY I WAS ABUSED AND NOW IN AMERICA ACCUSED.
ALL THROUGHOUT EUROPE, I AM WIDELY MISUSED.
DELIBERATELY IMPORTED INTO THE U.S.,
I WASN'T MEANT TO CAUSE SUCH GRIEF AND DISTRESS.

NOW WITH ALL MY ADDICTION,
I CAN CERTAINLY CAUSE YOU DISEASE AND CONFLICTION.
I'VE PROVED MY WAY FROM CITY TO CITY
OBVIOUSLY, DISRUPTING YOU WITH SELF PITY.
I HAVE BECOME A JOYOUS THRILLER;
I'VE PUT YOU IN A CAR AND YOU BECAME A KILLER.

ONCE IN YOUR LIVER, TORMENTING YOUR BRAIN,
YOU'LL CURSE ME FOR THAT TREMBLING PAIN.
HENCE, I AM ALWAYS FOR SALE.
REMEMBER MY NAME AND USE ME WELL...
YOU'VE HEARD MY WARNING --- IT'S YOUR DECISION;
I'LL PROMISE YOU INSANITY, DEATH, OR PRISON.

SNIPPETS

ACTS OF THE APOSTLES

"FOR JOHN TRULY BAPTIZED WITH WATER, BUT YOU SHALL BE BAPTIZED WITH THE HOLY SPIRIT NOT MANY DAYS FROM NOW."

THEREFORE, WHEN THEY HAD COME TOGETHER, THEY ASKED HIM, SAYING, "LORD, WILL YOU AT THIS TIME RESTORE THE KINGDOM TO ISRAEL?"
AND HE SAID TO THEM, "IT IS NOT FOR YOU TO KNOW TIMES OR SEASONS WHICH THE FATHER HAS PUT IN HIS OWN AUTHORITY."
"BUT YOU SHALL RECEIVE POWER WHEN THE HOLY SPIRIT HAS COME UPON YOU; AND YOU SHALL BE WITNESSES TO ME IN JERUSALEM AND IN ALL JUDEA AND SAMARIA AND TO THE END OF THE EARTH.".
OUT OF PRISON . .
"GO, STAND IN THE TEMPLE AND SPEAK TO THE PEOPLE ALL THE WORDS OF THIS LIFE."
AND WE ARE HIS WITNESSES TO THESE THINGS, AND SO ALSO IS THE
HOLY SPIRIT WHOM GOD HAS GIVEN TO THOSE WHO OBEY HIM.

THE ALCOHOL DEATH

LET ME TELL YOU ABOUT THE ALCOHOL DEATH
I'VE HEARD IT ALL WITH A SILENT BREATH.
THIS TIME I PASSED OUT IN A CITY JAIL;
I FELT MY BODY FLUSHED AND PALE.
I JUST KNEW I WAS ABOUT TO DIE;
CRAVING THAT ALCOHOL I KNOW THE CAUSE WHY.
WITHOUT THE WILLINGNESS TO QUIT,
 LACKING NO WILLPOWER,
 I'D AWAKE EXPERIENCING A FIT.
SEEMS LIKE I HAD TO DRINK EVERY NIGHT AND DAY;
I WASN'T READY TO ADMIT THAT I HAD TO ONLY PRAY.
AFTER MANY YEARS OF ABUSE,
I LOST EVERYTHING AND HAVE NO EXCUSE.
 I FINALLY BECAME SICK AND LOST ALL MY PRIDE; THEN
REALIZED I HAD TO CHOOSE AND DECIDE.
 HAD TO DO IT FOR MYSELF AND WENT TO MY KNEES AND
BEGGED THE LORD TO RID ME
 OF MY WAYS AND MY DISEASE.
TODAY I'M SOBER AND CLEAN.
I THANK THE LORD FOR NOW MY NEW LIFE IS
SPIRITUALLY SERENE.

SEEMS TO ME

IT SEEMS TO ME WE HAVE ALL PRAYED FOR THE LONGEST TIME ABOUT THE SITUATIONS WE'RE IN OR GOING THROUGH. YET, SOME OF US DO VERY LITTLE OR NOTHING TO CHANGE IT. MAYBE WE TAKE PRAYER FOR GRANTED. IF SO, THEN HOW CAN WE RELATE BEING OBEDIENT TO OUR LORD'S WAY? WE SOMETIMES COMPLAIN ABOUT THE WORLD AND ALL THE NEGATIVE THINGS THAT TAKE PLACE BUT SEEM TO FORGET THAT HIS WAY ARE NOT OUR WAYS AND HIS THOUGHTS ARE NOT OUR THOUGHTS. THOUGH HE KNOWS OF ALL OUR ACTIONS AND INTENTIONS PERSONALLY, KEEP IN MIND THAT THE VERY THING HE GAVE US TO USE TO CHOOSE AND DECIDE. DEPENDING ON HOW WE TAKE THE RESPONSIBILITY FOR OURSELVES DEPENDS ON OUR REWARD.

IF WE WANT TO COMPLAIN OF THINGS, THEN WE SHOULD BE WILLING TO DO OUR OWN PART. KEEP IN MIND, ALSO, THAT OUR CHILDREN LEARN FROM US --- WE LEARN FROM GOD AND OUR OWN MISTAKES. THEREFORE, WE ARE RESPONSIBLE FOR OURSELVES.

DON'T LET THAT DEVIL DANCE

I, ALONE, LET HIM DANCE;
I PLAYED WITHIN HIS ROMANCE.
THOUGH MY BODY DID NOT BE SINGED,
I WAS DETERMINED WITH THE LORD TO SURRENDER,
START OVER, AND BEGIN AGAIN.

I NOW DO REALIZE, WITH WISDOM AND PRAYER,
LIVING WITH THE DEVIL, WOKE UP AND NOW AM AWARE.
FOLLOWING THE LORD LIKE A CHILD, I MUST BE AWARE.

THE GOOD LORD REALLY KNOWS THAT I CARE.
UPON MY SURRENDER
HE PROMISES HE WILL FOREVER BE WITH ME,
AND WITH MY CHOICE I REALIZE I DIDN'T ALLOW LIFE TO
BE FAIR. TAKE HEED!!!
HE'LL PROVE YOU NO ROMANCE.
IF YOU FOLLOW THAT DEVIL, YOU'LL HAVE NO OTHER
CHANCE.

THE PREACHER'S HAND

PLEASE SIT DOWN AND HEAR WHAT I HAVE TO SAY.

WHAT AN EXPERIENCE!!---IT JUST HAPPENED THE OTHER DAY.

MY FIRST DAY HERE AS I RETURNED TO THE PEN, I WAS SILENTLY IN PRAYER.

I HEARD A VOICE, LOOKED UP, AND HEAVEN BEHOLD, A PREACHER MAN WAS STANDING THERE.

HE SMILED AND SAID,"EXCUSE ME! HOW LONG HAVE YOU BEEN PRAYING THAT WAY?"

I WALKED UP TO HIM IN MY CELL AND SAID, "PREACHER, EVER SINCE I'VE BEEN BAPTIZED; THAT'S BEEN EXACTLY ONE YEAR AGO TODAY."

WITH A SMILE WE SHOOK HANDS AND EXCHANGED A TIGHT EMBRACE.

THEN, THE PREACHER MAN ASKED ME IF I'D JOIN HIM IN GRACE.

HE PLACED HIS HAND UPON MY HEAD AS WE PRAYED; WE BOTH SPOKE IN AN UNKNOWN TONGUE.

IT CAME FROM OUR HEART AND SOUL AND FROM OUR LUNG.

AFTER WE FINISHED IN GRACE, THE PREACHER MAN HAD TEARS ALL OVER HIS FACE.

HE ASKED ME IF I KNEW WHAT I HAD SAID; AND I ANSWERED, "NO!"BUT, I HAD A VISION."

IT HAD TO DO SOMETHING WITHIN THIS PRISON.

THE PREACHER MAN SMILED AND PROUDLY SAID,
"YOU JUST RECEIVED A GIFT
THAT WAS SPIRITUALLY SENT FROM ME TO YOU.
I, TOO, HAD THE VISION. IT'S NOT UP TO ME. IT'S UP TO
YOU.
YOU MUST NOW FIND THAT SAINT.
IF IT TAKES FOREVER, YOU MUST HEAR HIS COMPLAINT."

THE PREACHER MAN LOOKED BACK WITH A TEAR-FILLED
SMILE AND SAID:
"I WON'T BE BACK FOR A WHILE. DO THE LORD'S WILL
AS I MUST LEAVE YOU BE;
FULFILL THIS VISION AND YOU'LL BE SET FREE."

IT WAS I WHOM THAT PREACHER MAN WAS TALKING
ABOUT.
IT'S ME, THERE IS NO DOUBT.

VIEWS OF A FRIEND

Greg found that returning to alcohol was, in reality, his false strength, the consequences of which were devastating. Greg had been searching for a comforter for years that would not disappoint him, and that comforter was next to him all the time. Throughout the first 38 years of his life, trouble obviously seemed to be everywhere he went. It was not until he discovered his Lord and Saviour, Jesus Christ, that the pieces began to come together. Now, Greg could see why he hadn't died the many times he overdosed or got into serious auto accidents. Now he can even see the blessing of being in prison to recover his sanity.

The poetry and prose in this book was written using the emotions of his real life experiences and situations. He had emotions so deep that many of us could not even begin to imagine the inner terror, terror and pain that deforms the insides of a human to the point that the individual cannot recognize himself. From these experiences he relates the works included in this book.

TRAGEDY, LONELINESS, TERROR, AND CONFUSION
ALL FROM THESE ADDICTIONS.

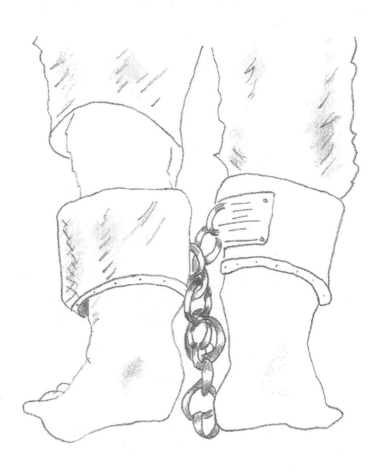

WHY ME, LORD?

I AM NOW FIFTY-FOUR YEARS OLD AND JUST RECENTLY HAVE AGAIN FOUND MY SPIRITUAL SELF. THAT WAS MISSING ALL ALONG. IT TOOK A LOT OF AFFLICTION BEFORE I WAS ABLE TO ADMIT MY ALCOHOLISM. MY THIRD WIFE, TERESA, HAS SEEN ME THROUGH A LOT OF DETOX CENTERS, JAILS, DEVIOUS BEHAVIOR, AND HOSPITALS. SHE NOW STANDS BY ME AS SHE SEES THE SPIRITUAL SIDE OF ME.

TODAY I FEEL AS IF I WAS RESCUED INSTEAD OF ARRESTED. AS MY FAVORITE HYMN SAYS IN "AMAZING GRACE", HE SAVED A WRETCH LIKE ME. FOR THAT I AM GRATEFUL. I HAVE ACTUALLY EXPERIENCED MY DEATH AT ABOUT AGE TWENTY-EIGHT FROM AN OVERDOSE OF HEROIN, SECONAL, AND ALCOHOL. I'VE SUFFERED FROM STROKES, JAUNDICE, AND HEPATITIS. I HAD MANY CHANCES. AS I LOOK BACK, I ASK MYSELF,
"WHY ME, LORD?"

TODAY I AM RESPONSIBLE TO CHOOSE AND DECIDE AS GOD GAVE ME THAT WILL. I HAVE BEEN BAPTIZED IN MY PENTECOSTAL CHURCH HERE IN SIOUX FALLS, SOUTH DAKOTA, WHERE I STILL FAITHFULLY ATTEND SINCE THAT TIME OF JULY 9TH, 1989. I HAVE FOUND MY REASON AND SPIRITUAL SELF. IT TOOK ME THIRTY-EIGHT YEARS TO GET HONEST WITH MYSELF AND NOW DOING MY BEST TO BE OBEDIENT TO HIM WHO SAVED ME. WITH THAT, I LIVE WITH A POSITIVE ATTITUDE THAT HAS CHANGED MY BEHAVIOR AND I NOW HAVE CONFIDENCE IN MYSELF AND, MOST OF ALL, AM DOING MY BEST TO BE A SPIRITUAL PERSON. I HAVE BEEN FORTUNATE TO WITNESS THIS TO YOU. TODAY I HAVE FAITH, IT BEING MORE VIGOROUS EVERYDAY. I'M NOT PERFECT AND AM BOUND TO MAKE MISTAKES; BUT WITH SINCERE PRAYER AND HONESTY, I AM ABLE TO BE THE FIRST TO CORRECT THEM.

NOW IT'S MY RESPONSIBILITY TO SHARE MY FAITH, STRENGTH, AND GRATITUDE BY SHARING THESE FEW PROSES WITH YOU. IN CONCLUSION THAT IF THERE IS A WAY, THERE IS A WILL. IT'S YOUR DECISION AS IT IS MINE. WE CAN ENDURE OR WE CAN REJOICE.

DAY BY DAY

DAY BY DAY I STAY CONFUSED
LOOKING THROUGH MY WINDOW WAITING FOR YOU.
IF YOU COULD ONLY BE SO KIND AS TO APPEAR IN MY
WINDOW
IF YOU'VE CHANGED YOUR MIND.
GIVE ME THE SIGN TO BRING US THROUGH;
FOR, LADY, I'M WAITING ON YOU. MY HEART IS SO COLD;
I NEED TO WARM IT BEFORE IT GETS OLD.
 I'M TIRED OF WASTING TIME.
 I CAN'T STAND HERE IN THE BLIND.
GIVE ME A SIGN THAT SHOWS ME YOU CARE.
 FOR, YOU, I'LL ALWAYS BE THERE.

PEOPLE MOVE LIKE CLOUDS

THEY'RE HERE TODAY AND FLOAT AWAY TOMORROW.
DRIFTING AWAY WITH SADNESS AND SORROW.
THEY WILL AIMLESSLY GET LOST IN LIFE EVERYWHERE
JUST TO FIND THEIR STRIFE.
ALL THROUGH THE NIGHT
EXPERIENCING LONELINESS WITH CONSTANT FRIGHT. IF
THEY DO FIND THEIR WAY BACK HOME,
THEY'LL COME WITH SHAME AND BE ALONE.
IT IS SAD BUT TRUE IF SOME DO MAKE IT BACK;
WE MUST REALIZE THERE WILL ONLY BE A FEW. ALWAYS
REMEMBER TO BE AWARE;
ACCEPT THE ONES YOU'LL SENSE THAT REALLY DO CARE.
WE ALL GET LOST AT TIMES IN OUR DAY;
JUST BE SINCERE WHEN YOU PRAY.
WATCH THAT CLOUD WITH PRIDE AND BE PROUD.

CALIFORNIA NUMBER: 78015

WELL BEFORE MY TEENS I WAS A WARD OF THE COURT.
NOT ONE INSTITUTION WAS ABLE TO COMPLETE A GOOD
REPORT.
MY PARENTS TRIED THEIR BEST TO RAISE ME UP RIGHT.
I REMEMBER BEING PUNISHED AFTER SNEAKING OUT ONE
LAST NIGHT.
I WAS SO SELFISH; I HAD NO RESPECT OR AFFECTION;
I NEVER REALIZED IT UNTIL MY FIRST EXPERIENCE OF
DETENTION.

THEN WITH REVENGEANCE ON MY MIND I ESCAPED WITH
A RESENTFUL HEART.
FOR A LONG TIME I HAD TO PLAY A FUGITIVE'S PART.
IT DIDN'T LAST LONG.
AT FOURTEEN I WAS SENTENCED TO A REFORMATORY.
FAILING MY ESCAPE ON A SIX-MONTH SENTENCE WAS THE
START OF MY TRAGIC STORY.

CONFINED IN A CELL, I BEGGED GOD TO FREE ME AND HIS
ANSWER WAS:

THE WAY YOU CARRY RESENTMENTS IN YOUR HEART
AND THE WAY YOU THINK,
YOU WILL BE BACK AND LEARNED NOTHING.
THEREFORE, YOU'LL RETURN SPIRITUALLY DEAD
AND BARELY ALIVE.
YES, YOU, NUMBER 78015.

SOUTH DAKOTA NUMBER: 25478

NUMBER: 25478 HAS FINALLY ENTERED THE PENITENTIARY GATE,
RELEASED FROM ISOLATION, STRONG WITH FATE.
ORDERS FROM THE WARDEN'S OFFICE, I'M ASSIGNED TO A CELL,
A LOT DIFFERENT FROM THAT IN JAIL.

THIS IS NOW MY ADDRESS, A NUMBERED CELL.
WHERE I'LL RECEIVE MY VISITS AND MY MAIL.
IT'SNOT VERY LARGE, JUST 6X10 FEET
WITH ALL MY POSSESSIONS I'LL WANT IT PROTECTED, COMFORTABLE, AND NEAT.
HANG UP MY FAMILY PHOTOS AND CONTEMPLATE ON MY PAST;
AND I'LL THEN REALIZE WHY I'M HERE, I WAS RUNNING TOO FAST.

I'LLTAKE PRIDE IN LITTLE WHAT I OWN;
I MUST BE CAREFUL FOR WHAT I GIVE OUT OR LOAN.
RATHER, IT BE MATERIAL OR ADVICE,
IT'S LIKE A GAME OF POKER OR PLAYING WITH DICE.
FOR IF YOUR NOT CAREFUL, YOU MAY LOSE YOUR RESPECT OR LIFE.

SO, DOING MY OWN TIME I'LL CONTROL MY STROLL
AND PRAY FOR MY SAFETY AND SOUL.
BEHIND THESE GRANITE WALLS I'M IN ANOTHER CITY
FILLED WITH CONVICTS AND SELF-PITY.

MAYBE JUSTICE WASN'T FAIR THOUGH NEITHER WAS I FOR NEGLECTING MY PRAYER.
I CALLED MY PASTOR ON THE PHONE AND ASKED IF HE'D HAVE THE TIME TO LOAN.
I WITNESSED TO HIM THAT I WAS HERE AND NEEDED PRAYER.
THEN HE SAID, "PATIENCE, I'LL BE RIGHT THERE".

WHEN HE ENTERED THE VISITING PLACE, WE HELD HANDS
IN PRAYER WITH A TIGHT EMBRACE.
NOW, WITH CONFIDENCE AND FATE
SOON CONTENTLY I'LL BE RELEASED FROM THE
PENITENTIARY GATE.

ME, NUMBER: 25478.

EXCUSE ME, WARDEN

PLEASE EXCUSE ME, **LET ME GO** -
I DON'T BELONG IN PRISON ANYMORE.

OH, WARDEN, WHAT HAVE I DONE SO WRONG?
THIS ISN'T WHERE I BELONG.
THESE CHAINS HAVE TORMENTED MY SOUL.
MY HEART HAS BEEN FROZEN AND IS COLD.

TO LIVE IN PRISON IS GETTING OLD.
EXCUSE ME, WARDEN, **LET ME GO**.
I'VE ALREADY SERVED TOO MUCH TIME
FOR SUCH A PETTY CRIME.

MY SENTENCE WAS TOO LONG, YOU SHOULD AGREE.
EXCUSE ME, WARDEN, **SET ME FREE**.

I HAVE CHANGED MY WAYS FROM SIN.
BELIEVE ME, I'LL NEVER RETURN AGAIN.
TO BE LOCKED UP FOREVER IS TOO SEVERE.
EXCUSE ME, WARDEN, **LET ME GO**.

I RETURNED ON A PETTY VIOLATION, YOU SHOULD
KNOW.
SO, WARDEN, EXCUSE ME AND **LET ME GO**.
EXCUSE ME, WARDEN, **LET ME GO**.

F

COU R AGE

E

E

E

D

O

M

20

ENDING A PRISON DAY

AS I END ANOTHER DAY HERE IN PRISON,
I HAVE THOUGHT OF MANY THINGS AND, MOST OF ALL,
MY EMOTIONS THAT HAVE ARISEN.
THE LONLINESS IS THE WORST BECAUSE OF THE
HEARTACHE
IT BRINGS WITH AN ACHING HEART AND MANY A SLEEPLESS
NIGHT.
I PRAY TO BE WITH MY LOVED ONES
AND SOON IT WILL BE ALL RIGHT.
WITH TEAR-STAINED PILLOW AND FLEEING MIND,
FEAR OF LOSING A LOVED ONE HAS LEFT MY SOUL IN A
BIND. THE CONSTANT FEARS I FEEL INSIDE
ARE NOT FEELINGS THAT ARE EASY TO HIDE.
MY FRIENDS PAUSE AND STARE,
BUT THE HURT IS SO DEEP THAT I DON'T CARE.
THEY ARE SINCERE WHEN THEY ASK, "WHAT'S THE
MATTER?" BUT, AS MY HEART IS BREAKING,
MY WORLD SEEMS TO SHATTER.
OH, JUST TO HEAR MY LOVED ONE'S LAUGHTER!
A LITTLE JOY IN MY GLOOM IS ALL I AM AFTER.
THE UNBEARABLE PAIN IN MY HEART IS NOT SOMETHING
NEW; BUT, THE FEAR FOR LOSING MY LOVED ONES,
"OH, GOD, WHAT SHALL I DO?"

DEDICATED PERSONAL HYMN
AMAZING GRACE

AMAZING GRACE, HOW SWEET THE SOUND
THAT SAVED A WRETCH LIKE ME. I ONCE WAS LOST
BUT NOW AM FOUND, WAS BLIND, BUT NOW I SEE.
T'WAS GRACE THAT TAUGHT MY HEART TO FEAR,
AND GRACE MY FEARS RELIEVED.
HOW PRECIOUS DID THAT GRACE APPEAR THE HOUR I
FIRST BELIEVED. THRO' MANY DANGERS, TOILS, AND
SNARES, I HAVE ALREADY COME.
TIS GRACE HATH BROUGHT ME SAFE THUS FAR,
AND GRACE WILL LEAD ME HOME.
WHEN WE'VE BEEN THERE TEN THOUSAND YEARS,
BRIGHT SHINING AS THE SUN,
WE'VE NO LESS DAYS TO SING GOD'S PRAISE THAN WHEN
WE FIRST BEGUN.

RELATED MESSAGE

All I knew was to con and connive
Constantly drank just to survive…
Thinking it was the only way to survive.

You may think you're confused

                          perhaps insane!
You must realize your obsession
Because that's what causes grief and depression.
It's all about drugs and alcohol…
Keep using and you may never comprehend this message at all.
Whatever you decide to do

                       Remember
It's all up to you
Blame it on poverty

              fame

                love

                   or sin…
Continue on and you may never hear this message again!

LOVER'S PRAYER

THIS LOVER'S PRAYER IS FOR YOU ALL THAT CARE.
WE, AS LOVERS, WILL BE TOGETHER
AND ENDURE HERE AND THERE.
WE ALL KNOW OUR HEARTS ARE NOT MADE OF PAPER
THOUGH THEY CAN EASILY TEAR.
SO, LET US ALL GET TOGETHER DOWN ON OUR KNEE
AND BE THANKFUL TO KNOW WHERE WE SHOULD ALWAYS
BE. WE SOMETIMES SAY WE DON'T LOVE ANYMORE.
WITHOUT REMEMBERING OUR VOWS
AS WE ENTERED OUR PREACHER'S DOOR.
WE MUST REALIZE WE DID IT TOGETHER
WITHOUT A DISGUISE AND WITHOUT A LIE.
IF WE MUST FAIL OUR VOW,
THEN LET'S RETURN TO THE PREACHER AND RENEW OUR
VOW. IT'S IMPORTANT THAT WE DO IT NOW.
THIS IS A LOVER'S PRAYER.
WE'LL INVITE OUR FAMILIES
BECAUSE THEY WERE ALWAYS THERE.
FOR THEM TO SHOW US THAT HOW MUCH THEY DID
CARE.
SO, BEFORE WE WALK BACK THROUGH THAT PREACHER'S
DOOR,
WE MUST REALIZE WHAT IT'S ALL ABOUT AND REALLY FOR.
WITHOUT A DOUBT WE'LL TRUST IN THE LORD
AND WITH OUR LOVER'S PRAYER,
WE'LL BE REUNITED HERE AGAIN
AND EVERYWHERE FOREVER MORE.

MAMA, I'L BE BACK

MAMA, I'M BACK HERE IN PRISON 'CAUSE I JUST WOULDN'T LISTEN.
SHE DONE ME WRONG AGAIN;
SHE'S OUT THERE COMMITTING SIN.
I KNOW, MAMA, THAT I SHOULD HAVE LISTENED TO YOU,
BUT WHAT IN THIS WORLD DID I DO.
I WON'T BE IN HERE THIS LONG OF TIME;
I DO KNOW I COMMITTED A CRIME.
I HURT HER BOYFRIEND AND DID IT GOOD
BECAUSE HE AND SHE KNEW I COULD.
MAMA, I SAID I'LL BE BACK AS I REALIZE WHAT I'VE DONE.
I REALLY THOUGHT SHE'D BE MY ONE.
SINCE IN HERE I'VE MET A NEW; SHE 'S JUST ONE OF A FEW.
I'LL BE OUT SOON AND BE WITH HER.
SHE TOLD ME TO BE WITH A CRIMINAL IS NEW.
SHE WANTS TO MEET YOU, MAMA,
BECAUSE SHE'S SWEET AND SHE WANTS TO.
SO, I'LL BE WITH YOU AND HER -- THAT'S WHAT I WANT.
I'LL BE HOME SOON AND YOU'LL MEET HER .
I KNOW YOU'LL KNOW SHE'S REAL AND TRUE.
THANK YOU, MAMA, FOR VISITING ME LAST TIME.
I'LL BE HOME SOON TO YOU. AND MY GIRL WILL BE MINE.
THIS I NOW KNOW WILL BE MY LAST TIME.
MAMA, I'LL BE BACK AND I'LL SPORT MY CADILLAC.
MAMA, I'LL BE BACK IN A FEW DAYS.
I'LL BE RELEASED. TRUST WHAT I SAY.
THANK YOU FOR YOUR LOVE AND TRUST;
TO BE BACK HOME WILL BE A MUST.
MAMA, I MAY BE CRAZY, BUT I'VE NEVER BEEN LAZY.
"I'M COMING HOME."
#25478 - I'LL KEEP MY CELL TIGHT AND WRITE ALL NIGHT.
I'LL CONCENTRATE ON MY CRIMES AS I SEEM TO COME BACK EVERY TIME.
I'LL FORGET THE WHISKEY, BEER, AND WINE;
JUST WRITE AS I DO MY TIME.

MY INMATES KNOW I'M SINCERE
AS I WALK UP AND DOWN THE TIER.
THAT'S #25478; WON'T BE TOO LONG
I'LL SEE THE OUTSIDE OF THE PENITENTIARY GATE.
THIS GRANITE WALL I'VE HAD ENOUGH
FOR I HAVE FINALLY SEEN IT ALL.
WHEN MY TIME DOES COME, I'LL RAISE MY HAND
AND LET ALL KNOW I NOW DO UNDERSTAND #25478.
MAYBE I'M SOMEWHAT CRAZY, BUT I'VE NEVER BEEN LAZY.
"I'M COMING HOME."

RIVER OF SNOW

(cocaine)

HERE AT THE RIVER, WE CALL THE RIVER OF SNOW,
HERE AT THE RIVER, THE SNOW GETS SO EXPENSIVE AND HIGH.
LOOK AT ME, BROTHER, I'LL TELL YOU NO LIE.

IT TOOK MY SELF-ESTEEM, IT MADE ME INSANE.
NOW I'M HOOKED; IT PROMISES ME DEATH; FIRST, I WILL SUFFER IN PAIN.
THERE WILL ALWAYS BE A PARTY. THE PARTY WILL GET SO HIGH.
THERE WILL ALWAYS BE A LOT OF PRETTY LADIES WAITING AND STANDING BY.
ALL READY FOR SKIING AND ALL WANTING YOUR MIGHTY BILL.
IF YOU HAVE THAT MONEY, SHE WILL SURELY SHARE YOUR THRILL.
THE PARTY IS ONLY TEMPORARY AND WILL COST A LOT OF DOUGH.
IF YOU CAN'T CHANGE YOUR LIFE, THEN I URGE YOU TO GO.

WHEN THE SNOW IS MELTING, YOU HAVE TO LET IT GO.
DICE UP THE MELTED AND GET YOUR LAST BLOW.
TAKE THAT MIGHTY DOLLAR AND GET DOWN TO THE STORE;
TAKE THAT LADY WITH YOU; YOU'LL SELL HER FOR MORE DOWN AT THE RIVER AT THE CORNER STORE.

THERE THE SNOW IS WALKED ON, STEPPED ON TO THE CORE.
THAT'S THE SNOW YOU WILL FIND THERE AT THE CORNER STORE.

AFTER YOU"VE TRADED YOUR LADY, YOU"LL HAVE NO RESPECT FOR MORE.
DOWN AT THE RIVER, YOU"VE BEEN ALL USED UP AT THE CORNER STORE.

YOU SAY YOU HAD A PROBLEM AND USED IT FOR A CRUTCH;
NOW YOU KNOW THE FIRST TIME YOU USED IT, IT WAS TOO MUCH.
IT"S TOO LATE AFTER YOUR CURIOSITY CAUSED YOU YOUR ADDICTION.
YOU WOULDN'T LISTEN, YOU KNEW IT WOULD PROMISE YOUR CONVICTION.

SHOULD YOU DECIDE TO RETURN TO THE RIVER OF SNOW,
STOP!...... IS IT REALLY WORTH IT, PERHAPS YOU"LL NEVER KNOW.

CONFINED PRAYER

O', LORD: LORD, I DON'T UNDERSTAND WHY THIS HAS HAPPENED TO ME
WHEN EVERYTHING WAS GOING SO WELL.

I DON'T WANT TO DIE THIS WAY --- I WANT TO LIVE.
I DON'T UNDERSTAND WHY I HAVE THIS DISEASE; BUT, YOU DO.

I KNOW YOUR WAYS ARE NOT MY WAYS AND YOUR THOUGHTS ARE NOT AS MINE.
I WANT TO BE OBEDIENT TO YOUR WAYS AND TO YOUR WILL.
IF IT IS YOUR WILL FOR ME TO LIVE IN A PRISON, THEN I ACCEPT.

I KNOW YOU'RE TRYING TO TEACH ME SOMETHING AND I'M TRYING TO LEARN.
PLEASE TAKE THE EVIL DESIRES AND THESE COLD SHACKLES FROM ME.

IF I SHOULD DIE IN PRISON, LORD, I WILL BE RID OF MY DISEASE.
THIS IS SOMETHING I'D BE ASHAMED FOR MY CHILDREN TO SEE.

TAKE THIS DISEASE THAT I ALLOWED TO CAUSE ME SHAME AND PITY.
I CAN'T GIVE UP; YOU'VE BROUGHT ME THIS FAR.

I WILL FIGHT THIS OBSESSION, LORD, BUT IT'S IN YOUR HANDS.
GIVE ME ONE MORE DAY WITH YOU, O',LORD.
I WILL PRACTICE YOUR WILL THAT I OWE TO YOU AND MYSELF.

JUST GIVE ME ONE MORE DAY

LETTER OF SINCERE

That prison, those jails, this poverty, the past
May pull us together forever and at last.
     The system may keep us temporarily apart,
But each visit and letter, Baby, brings me closer to your heart.
     It's hard to resist that telephone line
For your words are precious and so divine.
     Even though poverty guides me to the book for a loan,
Each and every day I seem to find a phone.
     Love: fret, not worry or doubt,
There's no reason to fear
     For when I offered you my love,
It will be with you, together or apart.
     From my heart and up above
You are the only woman I will love.
     I want you, I need you, I love you, I do.
My love is endless only for you.
     I propose myself not to forget this jail,
How uneasy the visits, phone, and mail.
     It won't be long now, Baby; our time is near.
Upon my release I'll prove my love sincere!

CONFINED PROMISES

THIS PRISON, THOSE JAILS, THE POVERTY, AND THE PAST
MAY PULL US TOGETHER FOREVER AT LAST.
THE SYSTEM MAY KEEP US TEMPORARILY APART,
BUT EACH VISIT AND LETTER BRINGS ME CLOSER TO YOUR
HEART.
IT'S HARD TO RESIST THAT TELEPHONE LINE
FOR YOUR WORDS ARE SO PRECIOUS AND DIVINE.
EVEN THOUGH POVERTY CAUSES ME TO FEEL ALL ALONE,
EACH AND EVERY DAY I SEEM TO FIND CHANGE FOR THE
PHONE.

DON'T WORRY, FRET, OR DOUBT;
WHEN I GIVE YOU MY LOVE, IT WILL BE WITH YOU,
TOGETHER OR APART.
MAY I PROMISE YOU ONE MORE LAST TIME,
I'LL ASK FOR HELP BEFORE I COMMIT ANOTHER CRIME.

I'LL PURPOSE MYSELF NOT TO FORGET THIS JAIL
HOW UNEASY THE VISITS, PHONE, AND MAIL.
IT WON'T BE LONG, FOR OUR TIME IS NEAR.
UPON MY RELEASE I WILL PROMISE TO YOU MY LOVE WILL
BE SINCERE.

D.A.K.O.T.A. SOUTH

I CAME OUT FROM SEATTLE;
THEY WOULDN"T LET ME DRINK THERE ON PROBATION.
OUT HERE RELAXING ON A BAR STOOL ENJOYING MY
VACATION.
I WOUND UP IN THEIR PRISON; THEY CAUGHT UP TO ME
TODAY.
IT IS A SAD SHAME -- I HAVE TO SPEND MY TIME HERE THIS
A-WAY.

IN THE SOUTH DAKOTA PENITENTIARY HERE IN SIOUX
FALLS
THE "D" IS MEANT FOR DRINKING AND THE "A" IS FOR
ALCOHOL.
THE "K" IS FOR KILLING, KILLING HALF MY LIFE AWAY.
THE "O" IS FOR OPTIONS; DRINKING I HAVE NONE AT ALL.
"T" IS FOR TIMING; IT WASN"T IN MY DAY.
"A" IS ON THE ENDING,
THE LAST LETTER TO SAY.
NOW I"M NOT JUST PRETENDING
WHEN I SAY IT"S A SHAME TO BE HERE TO STAY.

THAT SPELLS DAKOTA; IT"S HERE IN THE SOUTH.
NOW, YOU"VE HEARD MY WARNING -- COMING FROM MY
MOUTH.
SO, YOU KNOW HOW TO SPELL IT -- SPELL IT YOUR OWN
WAY.
HERE IN SOUTH DAKOTA, IT"S LAW HAS A LOT TO SAY.

IF YOU"RE ON PROBATION, YOU BETTER DETOUR THIS
TOWN
OR YOU"LL BE WITH ME WITH A GRIN AND A FROWN.
BUT, YOU MUST REMEMBER THERE'S A PRISON IN ALL OF
OUR STATES.

IF YOU PLAN ON DRINKING -- YOU"RE SURE TO SEE ITS
PRISON GATES.

D.A.K.O.T.A.

(WARNING)

I CAME OUT FROM SEATTLE RUNNING FROM PROBATION;
RELAXING ON A BAR STOOL ENJOYING MY VACATION.
WOUND UP IN THIS PRISON, THEY CAUGHT UP TO ME
TODAY. IT'S A SAD SHAME I HAVE TO SPEND MY TIME THIS
A-WAY IN   THE SOUTH DAKOTA PENITENTARY HERE IN
SIOUX FALLS. THE "D" IS MEANT FOR DRINKING
                AND THEN COMES THE BRAWLS.
 SO THE "D" REPRESENTS MY DRINKING
                AND THE "A" IS FOR ALCOHOL.
THE "K" IS FOR KILLING, KILLING HALF MY LIFE AWAY.
THE "O" IS FOR MY OPTIONS; I HAVE FEW AT ALL.
 "T" IS FOR TIMING; IT WASN'T IN MY DAY.
 "A" IS ON THE ENDING, THE LAST LETTER TO SAY --
AND WON'T BE PRETENDING WHEN I SAY,
" IT'S A SHAME TO BE HERE TO STAY."
THAT SPELLS DAKOTA, IT'S HERE IN THE SOUTH.
NOW YOU'VE HEARD THE WARNING COMING FROM MY
MOUTH. SO, YOU KNOW HOW TO SPELL IT -- SPELL IT YOUR
OWN WAY. HERE IN SOUTH DAKOTA ITS PRISON HAS A LOT
TO SAY.
IF YOU'RE ON PROBATION, YOU BETTER DETOUR THIS
TOWN
            OR YOU'LL BE WITH ME WITH A FOOLISH FROWN.
BUT, YOU MUST REMEMBER
THERE'S A PRISON IN ALL THE STATES.
IF YOU PLAN ON DRINKING,
YOU'RE SURE TO SEE IT'S PRISON GATES.

DEAR BEST FRIEND

DEAR BEST FRIEND, I WISH TO HEAR YOUR CALL.
YOU'RE ALWAYS ON MY MIND AS I MISS YOU MOST OF ALL.
THE OTHERS ARE JUST A CROWD
DRIFTING AIMLESSLY LIKE A LOST CLOUD.
HERE TODAY -- GONE TOMORROW
CAUSING NOTHING BUT GRIEF AND SORROW.
I MAY MISS A FEW AS THEY GET LOST IN LIFE,
BUT MOST IMPORTANT IT'S YOU I'M MISSING IN MY LIFE.

YOU'VE PROVED TO ME I AM ABLE TO LOVE AND FORGIVE;
WITH TRUST YOU GAVE ME A REASON TO LIVE.
THANK YOU FOR MY STRENGTH, MY FRIEND;
I'LL ALWAYS LOVE YOU AND WON'T PRETEND.
I AM GRATEFUL TO HAVE A FRIEND LIKE YOU;
THANK YOU FOR YOUR LOVE AND FORGIVENESS, TOO.

"SAME 'O GAME"

Girl, I thought you'd be true,
And I just fell in love with you.
I remember our first kiss,
And you know I just couldn't resist.
I wondered if you were just playing the part,
And you really tore me apart.
Why did you play me that way?
Now that you played me, you have nothing to say.
Do you play them all that way?
I now propose you to understand that you played the wrong man.
You can have your drugs and play your game
Because you know that you'll never to me be the same.
You'll end up living in shame.
I would have killed for you, but I got it together.
And, now I know what to do.
Now I found you out who you really are
And what you're all about.
I'd be a fool to love you and take you back ----
Girl, that's without a doubt.
You've got to get real because you should now know how I really feel.
You'll play the "same 'o game";
And, girl, you are not going to cause me to go insane.
So, go play your game and end up all alone.
Never play me or call me on my phone.
Just for advice, you can play your "same 'o game"
Because you'll never change.
Girl, go on your deceitful way
'Cause I don't have the time and do not want to play.
I'm now for real,
So now you do know how I feel.

BACK BEHIND THESE
PRISON WALLS AGAIN

BACK BEHIND THESE PRISON WALLS AGAIN INSIDE THESE WALLS WITHIN.
I'M WITH THE DEVIL, HIM AND I, HERE IN THIS CELL ALL ALONE.
BECAUSE I'VE FAILED MY RECOVERY AND FAITH, I ALLOWED THE DEVIL TO WIN.
I JUST HAD TO DRINK ONE MORE TIME; I DID IT ON MY OWN.
I FEEL LIKE I HAVE DIED GOD KNOWS I'VE TRIED.

I LET THE DEVIL TAKE MY DAY; I LET HIM HAVE HIS WAY.
NOW, MY FAMILY AND I WILL PAY THE DEBTS.
BECAUSE I DRANK AGAIN THE OTHER DAY,
I MUST FACE MYSELF WITH ALL MY REGRETS.

I FEEL LIKE I COULD HIDE AND CRY
THAN BE BACK BEHIND THESE PRISON WALLS AGAIN.
BUT, TODAY I'D RATHER DIE
IF I'M DESTINED HERE TO LIVE IN SIN.

AS I LOOK IN THE MIRROR, I SEE NO TEAR
AND MY FRIENDS TELL ME I'LL NEVER MAKE IT OUT THERE.
THOUGH I WALK PROUDLY DOWN THE CELL HALL, THEY ALL CAN SENSE MY FEAR.
I LIE TO THEM AND TELL THEM I JUST DON'T CARE.
SO, I MAY DO LIFE BEHIND THIS PRISON WALL.
THIS IS WHERE I MAY REMAIN.
AT LEAST I WILL BE FREE FROM THE ALCOHOL
BACK BEHIND THESE PRISON WALLS AGAIN.

FOR THIS I SHALL PAY A SEVERE DEBT, SURELY YOU CAN BET,
DWELLING IN THIS HOUSE OF SIN.

FOR THE REST OF MY LIFE HERE'S WHERE I'LL PROBABLY SIT,
BACK BEHIND THESE PRISON WALLS AGAIN.

"SEATTLE COUNTY JAIL"

Sitting in a cell in the Seattle County Jail
Driving with no license but, what the hell.
I made the mistake, but what did it take?
It took a lot 'o drinking without any thinking.
Now here ---- here to stay.

Takes just one more drunk driving without any striving.
The judge gives me a year just over some beer.
Takes my license as I drove without intention.
So, now I'm back in detention for not paying attention.

Here in this cell and not feeling well.
How much more will it take to understand my fate
Before I reach that prison gate?

Maybe there'll be a shot,
So I'll never again and never not.
If I keep driving, blacking out and not thinking,
I'm sure to see that gate.
For I know there's a prison in every state.

Fighting with the police and getting no release
Going to do a year so better get myself in gear.
Sleep all day ---- what can I say?
Stay up all night making my needles, making my ink ----
And tattooing alright.
Making my smokes
Still telling jokes.

If I want to stay out of jail at all,
Must have to forget all about the alcohol.
I am purposed to inculcate, for I can supplicate.
Stay off the booze and put my ride up for sale
So just maybe I can stay out of that dirty "Seattle County Jail".

SUMMER CITY JAIL

BACK AGAIN IN THIS JAIL WITH A DISGUSTING ALCOHOL SMELL.
NOW IN THE CELL THAT IS UNUSUALLY COLD,
THROUGHOUT THE INFESTED CORNERS WITH MOLD.
THE BUNK IS MADE UP OF SOLID STEEL, HARD AND COLD.
HOW UNEASY IT MAKES ME FEEL?
THE WATER TASTES WARM AND STALE.
THEY'RE ALL ALIKE, JUST ANOTHER JAIL.
THE GRAFFITI ALL OVER THE WALL I'VE SEEN IT MANY TIMES
AND READ IT ALL.
THE FOOD IS ONLY MEANT TO KEEP YOU ALIVE.
YOU MUST DEVOUR IT IF YOU WISH TO SURVIVE.
THE JAILERS YOU'LL FIND SOME GOOD AND SOME SAD.
BELIEVE YOU ME, THEY'RE NOT ALL BAD.
ALWAYS LISTENING FOR A KEY,
WAITING FOR THE DAY I'M RELEASED FREE.
THIS IS "SUMMER CITY JAIL" SO, **TAKE HEED**!!
I KNOW I'LL RETURN BECAUSE OF MY ALCOHOL GREED.

READERS, READ THIS WELL
FOR I PRAY YOU DON'T END UP IN THIS HELL!!

SIDE STREET AFFAIR

AS I WONDER UP AND DOWN THE STREET,
LET ME TELL YOU THEY AIN'T SWEET.
I CAME ACROSS A LADY NAMED CHERYL;
SHE STOOD TALL, BEAUTIFUL, AND NARROW.
I YELLED HER NAME AS SHE LOOKED BACK;
SHE LOOKED SWEET AND THAT'S A NATURAL FACT.
I WANTED TO TAKE HER TO MY HOME
SO WE COULD BE TOGETHER AND TALK ALL ALONE.
I'D TELL HER THAT I WOULD LOVE YOU
BECAUSE GREGORY WOULD BE TRUE.
AND, CHERYL, THAT'S JUST WHAT I'D DO.
IF YOU COME TO MY HOME, I'LL TREAT YOU RIGHT;
I'D HOLD YOU CLOSE WITH MY SOUL AND WITH ALL MY
MIGHT.
CHERYL, BELIEVE ME WHAT I'LL SAY AND DO
BECAUSE, LADY, YOU'RE THE ONE I WANT FOREVER AND
TO SHARE WITH YOU.
IF YOU INVITE ME INTO YOUR LIFE,
THEN I'D PROPOSE MYSELF TO BE RIGHT THE REST OF MY
LIFE.

SAD BUT TRUE

I want you out of my mind
Here and forever all of the time.
Release me, Kathy, and let me go;
I don't love you anymore, and I know you know.
I have to start over again.
You aint mine ---- it's my time.
I've found someone new,
And this song is just for you!
I can't take no more of your lies and alibis ----
And you do know why.
I wish you luck and a new life,
But always remember you put me through misery and strife.
I now found a new wife.
Your eyes of temptation are only aggravation.
So, now I end this song without blame.
Kathy, because we'll never be the same.
They that know it's a sad but true shame.

WE WALKED TEN MILES
IN OUR MOCCASINS

WE KNOW YOU WALKED WITH US BEFORE;
YOU SAVED US WHEN YOU KNOCKED UPON OUR DOOR.
WE ARE NATIVE AMERICANS, AND THAT'S WHAT WE STAND
FOR. LET US UNITE AS WE LOVE ONE ANOTHER.
FOR WE'LL ALWAYS BE TOGETHER
BECAUSE WE ARE THE BROTHER
AS WE CARE FOR EACH OTHER.
I FOUND THIS OLD WRINKLED-UP WHITE MAN ON MY
ROSEBUD RESERVATION.
HE WAS TRUE WITH NO HESITATION.
WE WELCOMED HIM IN OUR RESERVATION DIRECTION. I
TOOK OUT MY CAR, TROUBLE FOUR.
THOUGH THAT WHITE MAN PUSHED THE CAR,
HE DID NOT KNOW HOW FAR.
WALK TEN MILES IN OUR MOCCASINS
 BECAUSE WE ARE NATIVE AMERICANS.
AS WE NEED NO CAR, THE BUFFALO WATCH US AS STAND.
THOUGH MY BROTHERS, WE KNOW WHERE WE STAND.
SO, JUST WALK THAT TEN MILES
BECAUSE WE'LL LOVE ONE ANOTHER FOR LIFE
 AS WE WALK THAT MILE.

CLEAN AND SERENE

CLEAN IS WHAT WE CAN BE,
SERENE IS ALL ABOUT BEING WITH SERENITY
 AND LIVING DAILY CLEAN.
CLEANLINESS IS IN THE HEART,
AND BEING WHAT WE CAN SEE AND BE.
THE GOOD LORD WILL ALLOW US TO PROVIDE -
ONLY IF WE INDIVIDUALLY DECIDE.

WE MAY NOT DO IT ALONE,
BUT IF WE PRAY DAILY,
 THE GOOD LORD WILL BLESS US TO HAVE
 THE WORD TO SHARE TO SAY IN OUR HOME.
WE ALL DO CARE FOR EACH OTHER.
ONLY IF WE STAY CLEAN AND PRAY,
MAY CONTENTMENT BE WITHIN OUR HEART -
IF NOT, WE WILL FALL APART.

THIS IS SOMETHING WE MUST SHARE.
LET US REMAIN CLEAN AND SERENE.

WHY WHAT WE DO

YOU DID NOT CAUSE OUR BREAKUP;
NOW I ADMIT MY WRONGS.
AS I BLESS YOU, I REALIZE WHERE I NOW BELONG.
ALL ALONE AND LIVING BY MYSELF,
I WILL NOT BOTHER YOU ON THE PHONE.
I APPRECIATE YOUR CONCERN,
THOUGH YOU TAUGHT ME AS I DID LEARN.
I THANK THE LORD FOR YOUR FRIENDSHIP
            AS YOU'RE MY BEST FRIEND FOREVER.
WE ARE HONEST WITH OUR FRIENDSHIP.
FORGIVE ME AS I GO MY WAY.
NOW TO THIS DAY I WALK AND PRAY.
WHEN MY DAY IS GONE, KEEP MY WRITING
                WHERE IT NEEDS TO BELONG.
FORGIVE ME, TERESA, AS I DID WRONG.
YOU MUST UNDERSTAND THE LORD IS ALWAYS WITH YOU
AND THAT'S WHERE YOU BELONG.

GOD BLESS YOU!

WHY MUST WE HURT?

WHY DO WE HAVE TO HURT OURSELVES?
THE ANSWER WE DO NOT COMMUNICATE.
THEREFORE, WE DO CARE FOR ONE ANOTHER,
AND WE MUST STIPULATE; AND MOST IMPORTANT,
WE MUST CONVERSATE.
GUILT AND JEALOUSY WE CANNOT SEE AS WE ARE BLIND.
WE MUST PROPOSE OUR SELVES TO BE HONEST AS WE SEEK
AND FIND.
THE REASON WHY WE HURT IS BECAUSE THE GUILT AND
SHAME SET WITHIN;
THEREFORE, WE MUST REALIZE WE COMMITTED A SERIOUS
SIN.
THOUGH WE NEVER MEANT ANY HARM TO ONE ANOTHER,
LET US LIVE TOGETHER AS SISTER AND BROTHER.
SO, WHY SHALL WE LIVE WITH OUR PERSONAL HURT AND
LIVE WITH SORROW?
BECAUSE THERE MAY NOT BE TOMORROW.
LET LIVE AND ENJOY, STAND TOGETHER AS ONE
FOR WE'LL NEVER EXPERIENCE A DECOY.
SO, WHY MUST WE HURT WHEN WE LOVE ONE
ANOTHER?
REALITY PROVES WE BELONG
TOGETHER LOVING EACH OTHER.--
SO, WHY MUST WE HURT?

LAST ADVICE

JUST ONE MORE TIME -- I'LL TELL YA WHAT'S ON MY
MIND.
TODAY IT'S THE GOOD WORD YOU FIND IN YOUR BIBLE.
PEACE -- THAT I FIND.
IT'S THE WORDS THAT GIVE ME WISDOM,
AND THE PEACE FOR ME IS KIND.

JUST ONE MORE TIME
JUST ONE MORE TIME -- I'LL TELL YA WHAT'S ON MY
MIND.
TODAY IT'S THE GOOD LORD'S LOVE,
AND HIS PROMISE IS SO DIVINE.
I'VE TRIED ALL THE DEVIL'S WAYS;
IT KEPT ME FROM HIS PRAISE.
SO, I'LL TELL YA JUST ONE MORE TIME.

THE LORD PROMISED HE'D WASH AWAY MY SINS
AND EVERYTHING I'VE DONE.
I WAS LIVING ON NEEDLES AND PINS
AND DID A LOT OF WRONG UNDER THE SUN.
SO, YESTERDAY I TOOK A SOLEMN VOW
AND REPENTED ANYHOW.
TODAY I AM FREE NOW.

TODAY YOU CAN MAKE YOUR OWN CHOICE
AND HAVE A NEW LIFE AND BE CONTENT.
DO LIKE I; THEN REJOICE.
ALL YOU HAVE TO DO IS JUST REPENT.
HE'LL FORGIVE YOU OF ALL YOUR SINS.
HE IS SO FORGIVING AND KIND.
ASK HIM AND LET YOUR NEW LIFE BEGIN.
NOW, I'VE TOLD YOU WHAT'S ON MY MIND.

I'VE TOLD YOU FOR THE LAST TIME.

"THOUGHTS OF A LOCKED WORLD"

LOCKED IN A WORLD THAT NO ONE ELSE KNOWS;
WHERE YOU CAN'T EVEN SMELL THE SWEETNESS OF A
ROSE.
WHERE YOUR FEELINGS ARE WEAKENED
       BY THE ANGER IN YOUR MIND;
ALL YOU CAN THINK OF IS DOING YOUR TIME.

SOMEDAY YOU KNOW FREEDOM WILL COME;
THEN YOU'LL FEEL THE WARM COMFORTS OF THE SUN.

TIME IS WHAT YOU MAKE OF IT AND THE WISDOM TO
KNOW
       THE DIFFERENCE IS UP TO YOU.
SO, JUST KEEP IN YOUR MIND THAT SOMEDAY WHEN
YOU'RE
       READY, YOU WILL BE THROUGH.
LIFE IS WAITING OUTSIDE;
SO, DON'T BECOME WEAK AND IN THE BLUE.
YOUR EMOTIONS WILL STILL TELL YOU -- YOU STILL LOVE
       YOURSELF AS YOU.
TRY TO BE CONTENT AND CONTEMPLATE WHAT YOU
HAVE
       DONE THROUGH ALL YOUR MISTAKES.
JUST LEARN FROM WHAT YOU'VE DONE.
THEN, YOU WILL NEVER AGAIN HAVE FEAR TO BE ON THE
RUN.
SHOULD YOU NEVER BE LOCKED IN THAT WORLD
WITHOUT

THE SUN.

IS LOVING YOU WRONG?

IF LOVING YOU IS WRONG, I NEED NOT BE REAL
FOR WITH YOU I INTEND TO SAY AS I FEEL.
YOUNG LADY, MAY I EXPRESS THE REAL LOVE I HAVE FOR
YOU? MAY WE COMPROMISE FOR EACH OTHER
WITH A LOVE THAT IS TRUE?
THOUGH FORGIVE ME WHAT I SAY AND DO.
MY LOVE AND CONCERN WILL ALWAYS BE WITH AND FOR
YOU. IS THAT LOVING YOU WRONG?
ANSWER ME, YOUNG LADY, FOR I PRAY
WE TOGETHER WILL FOREVER BELONG.
IS THIS LOVING YOU WRONG?
IF NOT, IS IT WRONG FOR YOU AND I TO BELONG?
I BELIEVE OUR LOVE IS NOT TO BE ASHAMED
FOR YOU AND I WILL NOT TO BE BLAMED.
NOW, YOUNG LADY, IF LOVING YOU IS WRONG
MAYBE I'M JUST NOT FOR YOU TO TOGETHER BELONG.
IS THAT LOVING YOU WRONG?
YOUNG LADY, MY PRAYER MAY BE DEFAULTED
THOUGH IT'S YOUR DECISION AS LOVE CAN BE WRONG.
MY PRAYER IS "MAY WE BELONG?"
YOUR ANSWER WILL TELL ME IF THIS IS WRONG.
LET THE LOVE BE WRONG!
ONLY YOU CAN ANSWER THE TRUE
FOR THIS I'D RESPECT AND CHERISH YOU.

LOVE IS REAL

RESPECT ONE ANOTHER
AS WE COMPROMISE.
RESPECT EACH OTHER
AS WE MULTIPLY.
THAT'S WHAT LOVE IS ALL ABOUT.

BEDTIME EXCUSE

A COUPLE HAD GOTTEN HOME QUITE LATE AFTER A PARTY.
AS THE WIFE WAS GETTING READY FOR BED, THE HUSBAND
HURRIED INTO THE KITCHEN AND RETURNED WITH FOUR
GLASSES OF WATER AND TWO ASPIRIN. AFTER HE HANDED
THE PILLS TO HIS WIFE,
SHE ASKED, "WHAT'S THIS?"
"ASPIRIN," HE REPLIED.
"BUT I DON'T HAVE A HEADACHE, " SHE SAID.
"AHA!" ROARED THE HUSBAND WITH GLEE. "GOTCHA!"

YOU AND I

AIN'T IT FUNNY HOW BEES MAKE HONEY
AND HOW PEOPLE JUST WORRY ABOUT MONEY.
NO, NOT US! NO, NOT YOU AND I!
NOTICE HOW GRACEFUL A BIRD WILL FLY
AND HOW PEOPLE WILL GRIEVE AND DIE.
BUT, YOU AND I WOULD RATHER BE LIKE A BIRD AND FLY;
FLY UP TO HEAVEN -- WAY UP IN THE SKY.
JUST YOU AND I.
SO, WE'LL FORGET THE MONEY SINCE WE HAVE NONE.
WE'LL BE LIKE THE BIRDS AND BEES -- AND FLY --
FLY OUT OF THIS WORLD;
JUST YOU AND I.

HOT WOMAN

THERE IS A HOT WOMAN IN OUR CITY;
SHE SHOWS NO SELF-PITY.
SHE WALKS WITH UTMOST PRIDE;
YOU CAN SEE IT IN HER STRIDE.
BEING TALL, HOT, AND LEAN SHE'S A SENSUOUS SEX
MACHINE.   WITH LONG AND WAVY HAIR CONVERSATE
WITH HER
AND YOU'LL KNOW SHE DOES CARE.
SHE GOES BY THE NAME OF MICHELLE.
HER PRICE IS HIGH AND IS FOR SALE.
SHE HAS NO TIME TO CHANT AND PLAY
THOUGH FOR THE PRICE SHE WILL DO AS YOU SAY.
THAT'S THE HOT WOMAN IN OUR CITY,
SENSUOUS AND EXTREMELY RESPECTED AND PRETTY.

THE HOT WOMAN IN OUR CITY.

NOW THAT I KNOW YOU

NOW THAT I KNOW YOU MY LIFE I HAVE REARRANGED.
IT WASN'T EASY, THOUGH, BECAUSE OF YOU I HAVE
CHANGED.
I HAVE DRUNK TO YOUR LOVE AND CAUSED ONLY
SORROW.
THROUGH ALL OF OUR CONVERSATION, YOU'D REMIND
ME THE NEXTTOMORROW.

IT SEEMS I ONLY KNEW YOU IN AN ALCOHOLIC DAZE.
IT WOULD ALWAYS END IN A GRIEVING PHASE.
SOON AS I STOPPED FOR EACH OTHER, IT WOULD BE SUCH
A RELIEF
FROM OUR ARGUMENTS AND OUR GRIEF.
PUTTING US THROUGH SO MUCH SIN, I'D PROMISE I'D
NEVER DRINK AGAIN.
ALL WE SEEMED TO DO IS FUSS AND FIGHT, AND
LIVING IN PITY EACH AND EVERY NIGHT.

DRINKING ONLY TO EASE MY PAIN.
IF I HADN 'T STOPPED, I'D BE INSANE.
BEING SOBER OR BEING DRY, THE LIFE I FACE NOW IS WELL
WORTH THE TRY.
FOR ALL RESPECT AND CONCERN
IT TOOK ME A LONG TIME TO LEARN.

NOW THAT YOU KNOW ME . . . I KNOW YOU.

WELFARE BABY

I GOT A WELFARE BABY THAT IS SO FINE.
YOU KNOW THAT WELFARE BABY IS ONE THAT I CALL MINE.
SEEMS I'M ALWAYS DOING TIME,
IS WHY I'M KEEPING MY WELFARE BABY ON THE LINE.
SO, NOW IT WOULD BE A SIN IF I EVER CUT MY BABY THIN.

DONE WITH THESE FOUR MORE YEARS
WE'LL NEVER SHARE ANY MORE TEARS.
SENDING EACH OTHER MAIL WE SEEM TO ALWAYS TALK ABOUT
A LONG SAIL. SOON AS WE GET THE NOTION,
WE'RE GOING TO PACK UP AND CROSS THAT OCEAN.
WE'LL CROSS THAT OCEAN AND MAKE LOVE ALL IN SLOW MOTION.
NOW I'VE DONE ALL MY TIME.
I THINK I'VE GOT MY WELFARE BABY THAT I CAN CALL MINE.
LEAVING OTHERS ALONE,
I KEEP MYSELF BUSY ON THE PHONE.
I ONLY CALL THAT ONE BABY TO ASSURE HER I'M HER OWN.

YES, A WELFARE BABY I CAN CALL MY VERY OWN.
SHE IS SOFT AS SILVER WITH A HEART OF GOLD.
LISTEN TO MY STORY FOR IT WILL NEVER AGAIN BE TOLD.
I'M GOING TO TELL MY WELFARE BABY
THAT SHE'S COMING OFF THAT WELFARE ROLL.
ON THE PHONE I'LL TELL HER IT'S NOW THE TIME FOR A MIDNIGHT STROLL.
DOWN TO THE MIDNIGHT WATER
AND WE'LL POUR OUT OUR SOUL.
WE GONNA BUILD US A SHIP TOGETHER
AND CRUISE THE OCEAN IN ALL WEATHER.
WE'LL CRUISE THE MIDNIGHT OCEAN AND CRUISE IT SLOW.

FOR THE TIME WON'T MATTER; WE'LL CRUISE WITH THE
FLOW.
YES, I'VE GOT A WELFARE BABY, A WELFARE BABY OF MY
OWN.
WITH THAT BABY WE'LL STAY OUT ON THAT OCEAN AND
OFF THAT WELFARE ROLL.

YOUR STORY --- MY SONG

LISTEN TO ME PEOPLE; THIS DISEASE WILL CAUSE YOU
SHAME;
UNTIL YOU HOLD YOURSELF RESPONSIBLE, YOU ARE THE
ONE TO BLAME.
SOONER OR LATER WE MUST ALL SING OUR OWN SONG.
MY TIME IS NOW, I REALIZE WHERE I WENT WRONG.

I STARTED MY DRINKING I DON'T KNOW EXACTLY WHEN.
ALL I CAN TELL YOU IS, BECAUSE OF IT, I'M BACK IN THE
PEN.
AS MY ALCOHOLISM PROGRESSED, I COULD NOT FACE A
FRIEND.
I WAS TOO MISERABLE AND LONELY --- I'D LIE, SMILE, AND
PRETEND.

I MADE MY GEOGRAPHICAL MOVES FROM STATE TO
STATE
SUPPRESSING MY EMOTIONS UNTIL IT WAS TOO LATE.

I WOKE UP AS DOCTORS STOOD AT MY SIDE AND ALL
AROUND
WITH ELECTRODE PADDLES AND ALL STRAPPED DOWN.
SCREAMING AND YELLING WITH CONVULSIONS, I WAS ALL
IN KNOTS.
I CAME TO IN A PADDED CELL --- WAY UP ON TOP.

I CONNED AND I CONNIVED --- I PLEADED WITH THEM
ALL.
I WAS IN A HYSTERIA --- THEN I KNEW I WAS ADDICTED TO
THE ALCOHOL.

TRIED TO STAY SOBER ON MY OWN;
WOULDN'T TRUST NO ONE, NOT EVEN ON THE PHONE.
I DID SLOW DOWN, SLOWED DOWN TO A CRAWL;
TO REBUILD MY COURAGE, I HAD TO HAVE ANOTHER SIP
OF ALCOHOL.

I'M STILL ALIVE BUT BACK IN PRISON.
YES, I RELAPSED, IT WAS MY OWN DECISION.
NOW AGAIN I AM COMPETENT TO DEAL WITH MY MISTAKES
OUT THERE.
IT'S OBVIOUS MY ONLY ANSWER IS PRAYER.

I NOW BELIEVE IN THE SERENITY PRAYER.
I RECITE IT DAILY KNOWING MY HIGHER POWER DOES
CARE.
HE GIVES ME THE WISDOM TO CHOOSE AND DECIDE;
WITHOUT HIM I WOULD SURELY HAVE DIED.

I'M READY TO DANCE

JESUS, I'VE GOT ON ONE OF MY FAVORITE SUITS AND MY
DANCING BOOTS. I'VE GOT ON MY FAVORITE TIE.
I'VE GOT 'EM ON, THIS IS WHY:
I AM READY TO GO OUT AND STROLL. JESUS, SHOULD I
TAKE A CHANCE TO DANCE TO THIS GOSPEL BLUES AND
SOUL?
I'M READY TO SHARE MY LOVE.
JESUS, WON'T YA' GIVE ME A CHANCE?
I AM READY FOR A CHANCE TO LOVE.
ALLOW ME IF I SHOULD ASK FOR THIS DANCE.
AM I READY FOR A ROMANCE -- OR AM I READY FOR
LOVE?
HEY, NOW LOOK OUT THERE YONDER .
THAT LADY'S DANCING WITH ANOTHER MAN.
LOOK, HOW THEY WALTZ CLOSE AND WONDER!
AM I JEALOUS OR IS IT HER PLAN?
WHEN THE RECORD IS OVER, I'M GONNA ASK HER FOR A
DANCE
AND I'LL PROVE TO HER MY STANCE
AS I GIVE HER MY INNOCENT GLANCE.
WE'LL DANCE TO THE MUSIC WITH A 2-STEP SHUFFLE.
WHEN IT'S OVER, I'LL CALL YOUR NAME.
YOU KNOW I'M NOT ASKING FOR AN ORDINARY HUSTLE
BUT A CHANCE TO SHOW HER I HAVE NO SHAME.
JESUS, I'M READY TO DANCE.
I LEAD HER OUT ON THE DANCE FLOOR.
SHE SAID SHE WANTS TO KNOW ABOUT JESUS AND A LOT
MORE.
AS WE WERE DANCING, SHE WHISPERED IN MY EAR
AND AS THE DANCE WAS ENDING SHE SAID TO ME,
"IT'S ALL SO CLEAR AND WITH YOU I AIN'T PRETENDING."
JESUS, WE'RE READY TO DANCE.
JESUS, ARE WE READY FOR A ROMANCE?
JESUS, WE'RE READY TO LOVE.
BECAUSE OF YOU WE'LL ALWAYS BE READY TO DANCE.

GOOD NIGHT REQUEST

GOOD NIGHT TO YOU, MY DEAR.
ALWAYS REMEMBER I AM ALWAYS NEAR.
GOOD NIGHT AND PLEASE PRAY FOR ME;
AND YOU SHALL HAVE A VISION --- YOU'LL SEE ALL OF ME.

YOU'LL KNOW I'M PRAYING FOR YOU, TOO.
YES. JUST FOR US TWO.
I MUST REST FOR THERE ARE MANY MORE PRAYERS I MUST
FULFILL.
SO, KEEP YOUR FAITH AND PRAY
AND REALITY WILL SOON BE IN ALL OUR PRAYERS
FOR ANOTHER EACH NEW DAY.

FROM MY HEART'S BEST
THIS IS MY GOOD NIGHT REQUEST.

SPARKS FROM MY FINGERTIPS

LATE LAST NIGHT I WAS TAPPING ON MY TYPEWRITER
KEYS.
SHE WOKE UP AND TURNED OFF THE LIGHT AND SAID,
"COME ON TO BED. I WANT YOU, PLEASE."
I WAS SO SLEEPY THAT I SAW SPARKS FROM MY FINGER
TIPS.
SHE SMILED AND TOLD ME SHE'D PUT SOME SPARKS UPON
MY LIPS.
ALL I WANTED IS TO WRITE A SONG ABOUT HOW OUR
LOVE
WAS GOING WRONG.
SHE CARESSED ME WITH A GENTLE KISS AND SAID,
            "THIS IS NOT WORTH ALL OF THIS."
SHE SAID, "LET'S GO ON TO BED; AFTER TONIGHT YOU'LL
HAVE
            PLENTY TO WRITE ABOUT IN YOUR
HEAD."
I WANTED TO STAY UP ALL NIGHT.
NOTHING ELSE WAS ON MY MIND AS I ONLY WANTED TO
WRITE.
THEN, MY SPARKS FLEW FROM MY FINGERTIPS.
THEY JUMPED FROM MY HANDS TO HER TENDER HIPS.
I TURNED OFF THE TYPEWRITER AND THE BEDROOM
LIGHT;
WE WORKED OUT OUR LOVE AFFAIR ALL THAT NIGHT.
WE WOKE UP THAT AFTERNOON **AND**
REMOVED THE TYPEWRITER OUT OF THE ROOM.
SPARKS MAY FLY FROM THESE FINGERTIPS AS THEY WON'T
            BE FROM LACK OF SLEEP.
HER SONG WILL NOW COME TO ME ---

UNTIL THEN, I ALWAYS HAVE HER LOVE TO KEEP.

WHAT MONEY CAN'T BUY

MONEY WILL BUY A BED BUT NOT SLEEP;
BOOKS BUT NOT BRAINS;
FOOD BUT NOT APPETITE;
FINERY BUT NOT BEAUTY;
A HOUSE BUT NOT A HOME;
MEDICINE BUT NOT HEALTH;
LUXURIES BUT NOT CULTURE;
AMUSEMENT BUT NOT HAPPINESS;
RELIGION BUT NOT SALVATION;
A PASSPORT TO TRAVEL EVERYWHERE;
BUT YOU CAN'T BUY THE LORD!
OR
YOU CAN'T BUY YOURSELF 'CAUSE THE LORD WILL GIVE
WHAT YOU DESERVE AS YOU PRAY.
THAT'S WHAT MONEY WILL BUY AS THE ANSWER IS
PRAYER.

LAST RIDE WITH THE DEVIL

I WENT OUT DRIVING LAST NIGHT WITH MY HEADLIGHTS
GLOWING BRIGHT.
THE WARM NIGHT AIR ACROSS MY FACE RUSHED THROUGH
ME WITH A SOFT EMBRACE.

THE NIGHT WAS LONELY; THE ROAD WAS STRAIGHT; THE
TEMPTATION WOULD NOT LET ME WAIT.
MY MOTOR WAS WOUND UP TIGHT AND THERE WAS NO
OTHER SOUL IN SIGHT.
AT 120 mph I HELD THE BARS WITH A SUICIDE FROWN.
I TWISTED THE GAS PEDAL FARTHER DOWN.

I FELT THE EXCITEMENT RUSHING WITHIN ME AT A FAST
PACE, SEEMED LIKE FIRE UPON MY FACE.
THE ALCOHOL DAZE BLURRED MY VISION, THOUGH I
COULD SEE THE DEVIL WAS RIDING NEXT TO ME.

I TRIED TO TURN AWAY FROM HIM; THEN, SUDDENLY I FELT
A SHARP PAIN WITHIN.

I FELT THE GROUND; THE MOTOR STOPPED; THEN, I HEARD
SILENCE ALL AROUND.

I REMEMBER WIPING THE BLOOD FROM MY EYES TO SEE;
BUT ONLY TO VISUALIZE THE DEVIL RIDING NEXT TO ME.

I HEARD HIM LAUGH AND CALL MY NAME; I SAW THE FIRE
BUT FELT NO MORE PAIN.

THE SIGN AHEAD SPELLED PARADISE; TO FOLLOW HIM I'D
HAVE TO MAKE A SACRIFICE.

HE PULLED AHEAD, I SAW HIM WAVE, AND THEN I FOLLOWED
HIM INTO HIS GRAVE.

THE CONCLUSIONS OF DEVIANCE

CONTEMPLATING MY YESTERYEARS OF SOCIAL DEVIANCE,
I RESENTED SOCIETY, I THOUGHT THAT CAUSED MY GRIEVANCE.
ALWAYS DISOBEYED MY PARENTS AND AUTHORITY
TO PROTECT THE APPREHENSION OF MY INFERIORITY.
I ALLOWED NO TIME FOR MY EDUCATION;
TO SURVIVE I RELIED ON MY DEVIANT OBSERVATION.
MY DEFIANCE WAS OBSESSED IN CONFUSION AND ADDICTION
PHYSICALLY AND MENTALLY CAUSING DESTRUCTION AND CONFLICTION.

LATER IN LIFE I KNEW I HAD TO TRUST TO RELATE.
EXPERIENCED, TIRED, AND WISER, I LEARNED TO COMMUNICATE.
MY INCOMPETENT ATTITUDE HAD TO BE REARRANGED
BEFORE I COULD POSSIBLY BE CHANGED.
I CHANGED MY THOUGHTS AND ACTIONS ONCE I FOUND MY SPIRITUAL POWER.
I PURPOSED MYSELF WITH DISCIPLINE IN PRAYER AND IN EVERY HOUR.
NOW, WITH CONFIDENCE IN MY DECISION
I'LL ALWAYS BE FREE IN SPIRIT AND FROM PRISON.
DAILY, DOWN ON MY KNEES IN PRAYER AND BEING SINCERE,
I AM CONTENT THAT MY TOMORROW WILL FAITHFULLY APPEAR.

MAY THIS BE READ TO REMEMBER TO INSPIRE
WITH FAITH, TRUST, AND A DESIRE
TO HELP OTHERS IS SOMETHING THAT WE ALL SHOULD ADMIRE.

HOMELESS BONNEY'S TOMORROW

HER HUSBAND TORE THEM APART
AS HE TORE HER HEART APART.
THE ALCOHOL TELLS IT ALL.
A VICIOUS DISEASE THAT'LL NEVER PLEASE.
DOWN ON HER LUCK SHE WAS IN THE STREETS AND LIVING
UNDER A BRIDGE BARELY GETTING BY.
AS I HEARD HER STORY, SO UNFORTUNATE, I DO
UNDERSTAND WHY.
SHE IS ONE BEAUTIFUL LADY AND WILL GIVE WHAT SHE
HAS ANY GIVEN TIME.
IF YOU'VE BEEN THERE YOU WOULD KNOW BY HER
EXPRESSIONS AND REALIZE IT'S A LONELY SIGN.
AS I FOUND HER IN LONELINESS, SADNESS, AND FILLED
WITH SORROW, THE LADY THOUGHT SHE MAY NOT SEE
TOMORROW.
BONNEY HAS BEEN THROUGH SO MUCH PAIN, BUT SHE
NEVER LIVED WITH ANY GUILT OR SHAME.
I THEN PUT MY HAND UPON HER HEAD.
AS WE DID PRAY, SHE SPOKE TO THE LORD AND THANKED
HIM FOR THIS DAY. SHE NOW HAS FOUND A GOOD FRIENDLY
HOME THAT SHE NOW CAN CALL HER OWN. SHE NOW
ADMITS WITH THE GRACE OF GOD SHE'LL NO LONGER
EXPERIENCE ANY SADNESS, LONELINESS, OR SORROW.
EVERY DAY THERE WILL BE A BLESSING IN HER EVERY
TOMORROW.

"TERESA"

Why did we build it up from the start?
I do realize we're now apart.
Kathy and Crystal didn't do me right,
But with you, you have always been there and treated me right.
If I could have you back, I'd stay off the railroad track.
Because, Teresa, I know you're with someone new,
And now I just don't know what to do.
When a man loves a woman like I do you,
I realize, Teresa, I wasn't true.
Forgive me, Lady, and maybe you'll take me back
Now that I'm not running the streets and off the railroad track.
Men ain't supposed to cry.
But, listen to me for I'm asking for another try.
You may say, "Why?",
But I know we deserve another try.
I'll do you right and keep holding you with all my might,
And keep our love together and keep it right.
So, Teresa, let me know, so I'll know what to do and where to go.
If not, I'll know how to keep myself low.
Walk with experience and I'll walk slow.
You know I'll always love you; and if you take me back,
We'll never make another mistake and that's a fact.
Teresa, I do really love you.
I thank you for being you.

GRAND - SON

GRANDSON, I'M GONNA TELL YOU THE TRUTH ABOUT MY
PRISON DAYS.
YOUR GRAMMA AND I'VE BEEN SEPARATED FOR MANY A
DAYS.
I WOULD START DRINKING AND THEY'D TAKE ME AWAY.
GRAMMA WOULD JUST BOW HER HEAD AND PRAY.
GRANDSON, IF YOU START TO DRINKING, YOU'LL END UP
IN PRISON, TOO.
THIS I'M TELLING YOU BECAUSE I HAVE A LOT OF LOVE
FORYOU.
YOUR MOTHER - I PUT HER THROUGH A LOT OF MISERY
AND PAIN;
AT THAT TIME SHE WOULD SWEAR THAT I WAS INSANE.
GRANDSON, THIS IS SOME ADVICE FROM ME TO YOU.
TAKE YOUR TIME GROWING UP AND IN EVERYTHING YOU
DO.
DON'T DO LIKE YOUR GRANDPA DONE.
DRINK HALF YOUR LIFE AWAY JUST FOR A LITTLE SIN AND
SO . . .
TAKE YOUR TIME AND PAY ATTENTION IN LIFE.
GROW UP AND FIND A GOOD WIFE.
RAISE YOUR CHILDREN LIKE YOUR GRANDPA TRIED TO
DO.
DON'T DRINK AND JUST FOLLOW THE GOLDEN RULE.
THE DRINKING WILL PUT YOU IN PRISON OR YOU'LL GO
INSANE.
YOUR GRAMMA WILL TELL YOU I WENT THROUGH A LOT
OF SHAME.
DON'T DO LIKE GRANDPA AND DRINK HALF YOUR LIFE
AWAY.
I'M OUT OF PRISON AND I'M HERE TO STAY.
GRANDSON, THAT'S WHY I SERVED MY PRISON DAYS.

GRANDDAUGHTER'S SONG

I WOKE UP THIS MORNING WITH MY GRANDDAUGHTER
ON MY MIND
AND PRAYING TO THE LORD.
I WOKE UP THIS MORNING PRAYING FOR HER SOUL
AND THANKING JESUS FOR MY GRANDDAUGHTER.
SHE'S A SPECIAL GIRL.
THANK YOU, JESUS, SHE'S THE FAVORITE OF MY WORLD.

I WOKE UP THIS MORNING FEELING GRATEFUL FOR HER
MOTHER.
SHE'S MY DAUGHTER AND I COULDN'T REPLACE HER WITH
ANOTHER.
YES, SHE, TOO, IS A SPECIAL GIRL ALTHOUGH, AT TIMES,
SHE PUTS MY MIND IN A SWIRL.

I WOKE UP THIS MORNING THINKING OF ALL I'VE DONE
WRONG.
THOUGH I CAN THANK JESUS THEY, TOO, CAN NOW HAVE
A CHANCE IN THIS LIFE WITH A SPECIAL SONG.
I'LL NEVER FORGET MY GROWING UP; IT ALMOST TOOK ME
TOO LONG.

I WOKE UP THIS MORNING AND PRAYED FOR THEIR
GUIDANCE AND DIRECTION.
(WITH MY DAUGHTER NOW BAPTIZED), I'LL TRUST THAT
SHE'LL GO THROUGH HER LIFE BLESSED WITH CHARITY
AND AFFECTION.

I WOKE UP THIS MORNING FEELING FINE
PRAISING THE LORD.
THANK YOU, JESUS, FOR MY GRAND GIRL.
SHE'S ANOTHER PRAYER IN MY WORLD.

I WOKE UP THIS MORNING
PRAISING THE LORD.
I WOKE UP THIS MORNING WITH A SONG -- SINGING.

THANK YOU, JESUS.
WITHOUT YOU WE'D NEVER HAVE A REASON TO BELONG.

TRUE COUNTRY VIBES

K.X.R.B. IS MY COUNTRY FAVORITE.
BEST COUNTRY MUSIC!
ALWAYS PLAYING IT RIGHT FROM MORNING AND ALL
THROUGH THE NIGHT.
I'D BE A REAL LIAR IF I'D NOT SAY IT'S MY STATION AND
DESIRE.
KEEP PLAYING VINCE GILL; HE TELLS IT FOR REAL.
WE ALL NEED LORETTA LYNN;
KEEP HER SINGING AS WE LISTEN AND BEGIN.
ALAN JACKSON IS HERE IN THE REAL WORLD AND TELLS
US IT'S NOT EASY AT ALL.
WHEN WE GET DOWN , WE KNOW WHO TO CALL.
 K.X.R.B. IS THE BEST 'CAUSE WE'VE HEARD THE REST.
 LET THE COUNTRY GO FOR OUR LISTENERS ALL KNOW.
KEEP THE RADIO ON AS WE APPRECIATE THE MUSIC AND
WHAT YOU HAVE TO SAY. THEREFORE, WE TUNE YOU IN
EVERY MORNING, NOON, AND NIGHT.
THANK YOU, MCDANIEL AND THE CREW.
YOU ALWAYS KNOW WHAT TO PLAY AND DO.
COUNTRY IS ALL ABOUT LOVE AND CONCERN
AS WE BEEN THERE AND WILL STAY TOGETHER AS WE ALL
LEARN.
THANK YOU, K.X.R.B., FOR AIRING YOUR COUNTRY
STATION FOR US ALL AND INCLUDING ME.
YOU HELPED BRING BACK MY WOMAN TO ME.

ASPHALT JUNGLE

I FOUND MYSELF IN SAN BERNARDINO
EXPERIENCED WITH THE HOMELESS AND KNEW WHAT
THEY DO. WE ALL CONGREGATE WHAT IS KNOWN AS THE
"BEER STOP,"
THE CITY BUS BENCH WHERE WE SIP ON OUR KING COBRA
BEER THAT NEVER HAS A TOP. MET A MAN KNOWN AS
CONNIVER;
HE PROVED HIS SELF AS A NATURAL SURVIVER.
HIS NAME WAS LARRY AND HE SHOWED ME HIS WAYS
AND HELPED ME TO SURVIVE ALL THROUGH THE DAYS.
THE ASPHALT JUNGLE IS ABOUT THE STREET;
IT GETS COLD AND LONELY AND ISN'T SWEET.
BEING DISABLED I AM FORCED TO PANHANDLE FOR A
DAILY MEAL READING THIS YOU COULD IMAGINE HOW
WE FEEL.
THE ASPHALT JUNGLE IS WHAT WE WELL KNOW;
JUST ASK LARRY HE WOULD DIRECT YOU AND SHOW YOU
THE RIGHT CORNER TO GO. THE ASPHALT JUNGLE IS NOT
TO BE;
BEFORE YOU CRITICIZE US, JUST LIVE IT AND YOU'LL SEE.
IF YOU GO HUNGRY FOR A GIVEN DAY,
STOP AND LOOK FOR WE DO PRAY
THAT IS THE ASPHALT JUNGLE WAY.
THIS WAY OF LIFE,
IS NO WAY TO BE FOR IT'S ALL ABOUT SADNESS AND STRIFE.
LARRY MAY BE AN INNOCENT CONNIVER
THOUGH HE BELIEVES IN THE LORD AND IS A SURVIVOR.

IN RESPECT OF LARRY D WIDAWSKI

BLACK TRAIN (HEROIN)

BLACK TRAIN -- YOU PULLED ME DOWN.
WHATEVER THE REASON IT SEEMS I'M ALWAYS BOUND
AND YOU'RE EASILY FOUND AROUND.

BLACK TRAIN --TRAIN OF TAR;
FIX IT UP AND I'LL GO FAR.
YOU LIED, CHEATED AND STOLED;
BUT NO MATTER WHAT, THIS STORY HAS TO BE TOLD.
YOU DID LEAD ME ASTRAY AND ONE MORE TIME I HAD TO
PRAY. YOU GOT INTO MY VEIN; NOW I KNOW I'M INSANE.
CAN'T THANK YOU, THOUGH, IT'S NOTHING NEW;
BLACK TRAIN -- IF I ONLY KNEW.
BLACK TAR -- TAR OF HEROIN, YOU DID ME WRONG,
BUT IF I ONLY KNEW YOU'RE THE ONE THAT I ALWAYS
DID   CRAVE,
I'D BELIEVE WHEN YOU'D PROMISE ME A GRAVE.
NOW WITH HEPATITUS "C", YOU CAUSED ME TO BELIEVE.
I HAVE TO JUMP OFF OF YOUR TRACK
AND, HEAVEN FORBID, I'LL NEVER BE BACK.
I NOW REALIZE WHAT YOU'VE CAUSED ME.
THANK GOD HE WOKE ME WITH PRAYER AND HE ALLOWED
ME   TO SEE.
GOOD BYE, BLACK TRAIN -- GOOD BYE FORVER
I'LL NOT TASTE YOU WITH MY SHORT LIFE;
I'LL DAILY THANK GOD AND RELIVE MY LIFE IN SERENITY
AND FAITHFUL STRIFE.

"MY DREAM OF HER"

FAINTLY REMEMBERING FALLING ASLEEP,
THIS DREAM I'LL ALWAYS CHERISH AND KEEP.
SUDDENLY I SAW HER A SUMMER MORNING;
SHE TURNED TO ME AND STARED WITH NO WARNING.
I ASKED HER IF SHE IS GOING MY WAY;
THEN PATIENTLY WAITED TO HEAR HER SAY, "I'M OUT FOR
A WALK FOR THE DAY, AND, YES, I AM GOING YOUR WAY."
SOON AS I ASKED HER NAME, I FELT MY HEART;
IT FELT LIKE A FLAME.
WE WALKED HAND IN HAND, TALKING AND LAUGHING,
KICKING THE SAND.
SEEMS WE WALKED MILES ALONG THE BEACH;
ALWAYS CLOSE TOGETHER IN REACH.
SHE WAS BEAUTIFUL AND SHY;
I'LL ALWAYS REMEMBER HER UNTIL THE DAY I DIE.
SHE HAD A SENSUOUS SMILE AND PRECIOUS LIPS,
SO UNDERSTANDING WITH HER SOFT FINGERTIPS.
I REACHED OUT TO TOUCH HER;
THEN SUDDENLY I CAME TO A BLUR.
AS I OPENED MY EYES IT SEEMED SHE DISAPPEARED INTO
THE MORNING SKIES.
I ONLY WISHED I COULD FALL BACK ASLEEP
FOR THIS DREAM I'LL ALWAYS KEEP.
NOW I KNOW I STILL HAVE A DREAM.

IF WE CARE

BABY, IF YOU HAVE THE TRANQUILITY,
THEN YOU MUST HAVE THE RESPONSIBILITY.
MAY I PROPOSE YOU TO KNOW I HAVE IN YOU THE FATE.
YOU SAY YOU DO CARE;
THEREFORE, YOU MUST STIPULATE TO ME, BABY, THAT
        YOU CARE FOR ME ONLY AS I DO YOU.
FOR THIS REASON WE MUST CONTEMPLATE TOGETHER
        WITH LOVE AND WITH ALL OUR FATE.

MY SISTER AND I

WE WERE BORN IN POVERTY.
SEEMS IT WAS MY SISTER AND ME,
THOUGH MY MEMORY IS OF MY SISTER, DONNA MARIE.
SHE IS THE SISTER THAT HELPED ME SEE;
HER NAME IS DONNA MARIE.
SHE IS THE SISTER THAT MADE ME SEE.

SHE HELPED ME TO REALIZE TO UNDERSTAND
RIGHT FROM WRONG AND OF GOD'S PLAN.
WE'VE PLAYED TOGETHER AND FOR EACH OTHER;
AND, FINALLY REALIZED WE HAD THE SAME MOTHER.
NOW WE ARE OLDER WITH A LIFE OF OUR OWN;
I SEEM TO ALWAYS CALL HER WITH A DRUNKEN TONE.

THE NEXT DAY I WOULD CALL HER TO APOLOGIZE;
THEN THAT'S WHEN SHE'D MAKE ME REALIZE.
I'VE WORKED WITH HER HUSBAND WITH TRUE
CONCERN
BECAUSE HE ALSO TAUGHT ME WHAT I COULD LEARN.
WE PRAY WE'LL NOT BE IN POVERTY ANYMORE
FOR HE AND MY SISTER INFORMED ME OF THE SCORE.

I KNOW WE MUST STAND TOGETHER
NO MATTER WHAT THE SITUATION OR THE WEATHER.
WE'VE BEEN THROUGH GOOD AND BAD
AND REALIZE HOW MUCH I LOVE THE FAMILY
AND WHAT I COULD HAVE HAD.
IF THESE WORDS ARE TRUE,
I MUST SHOW MY FAMILY WHAT I CAN DO.
THAT'S

MY SISTER AND I.

CALVERT WHISKEY

TUNING IN ON THE RADIO UP HERE IN MY PRISON CELL,
I CAN'T MAKE A PHONE CALL; SO, I'LL CONTACT YOU BY
MAIL.
LISTENING TO OUTLAW COUNTRY ON 102 F.M.(K.T.W.B.),
FLUSHED OLD CALVERT DOWN; NOW,
I REALIZE WHAT I COULD BE.

IF I COULD CALL IN TO DEDICATE A SONG,
IT WOULD GO OUT TO MY FRIENDS TO EXPRESS THAT
WHEN I DRANK YOU'D KNOW I WAS WRONG.
I USED TO LISTEN TO YOU UPON A BAR STOOL.
CAN'T BLAME IT ON THE DRINK OR MUSIC;
IT WAS JUST ME PLAYING THE FOOL.

THE ADVERTISEMENTS ARE GOOD AND SO IS THE LOCAL
NEWS.
THOUGH I SURE APPRECIATE IT WHEN YOU PLAY THE
CLEAN COUNTRY BLUES.
THE SWING IS IN AND THE TWO-STEP IS GRAND.
THAT'S WHERE MY HEART IS OUT THERE IN OUTLAW
COUNTRY LAND.
I LISTENED TO THE OLDIES UNTIL I FLUSHED THEM
DOWN.
NOW, I'M LISTENING TO THE COUNTRY AND LIKE IT WHEN
YOU CLOWN.
IT PUTS ME IN A HUMOROUS LIFE AND REMINDS ME OF THE
GOOD TIMES OUT THERE WITH MY WIFE.
I LISTENED TO CALVERT BUT DIDN'T PAY NO MIND TO HIS
FIRST NAME.
IT FINALLY SOAKED IN AFTER I WAS DROWNED IN SHAME.
THOUGHT I COULD DANCE AS I DRANK TO HIS FLAME.
NOW, I'LL PAY ATTENTION TO HIS FIRST NAME.
A DEDICATION NOW COMES TO MIND:

HAVE MERCY THAT FITS TO THE TIME
OR ANYTHING WITH THE LORD THAT'LL

KEEP ME FREE.

SO, FLUSH THAT STOOL AND PLAY ME A TUNE
OUT TO MY WIFE AS I'LL GET BACK IN CONTACT SOON.
THANK YOU FOR YOUR COUNTRY AND ALL YOU DO.
YOUR REQUEST LINE IS GREAT AND I'LL KEEP ON KEEPING
YOU.
PLAY THE OLD ONES AND CONWAY WITH LORETTA, TOO.

ME AND BEVERLY

THIS IS ABOUT ME AND BEVERLY
 AND I JUST HAD TO FIND OUT TO SEE.
THAT'S ME AND BEVERLY.
IF YOU MAY KNOW, WE JUST CLOSED OUR DOOR.
WE AGREED AND UNDERSTOOD.
YES! YOU AND WE ALL DO KNOW
WHAT IT'S ALL ABOUT AND ALL FOR.
WE HAD A GREAT TIME JUST HER AND ME.
JUST ME AND BEVERLY.
I ALL ALONG SENSED SHE WAS ALL MINE.
SHE SHOWED ME TENDERNESS AND SOUL
 SO WE JUST ROCKED AND ROLLED.
WE JUST SPENT TWO DAYS,
AND YOU DO KNOW WHAT THIS SONG WANTS TO SAY.
WE DID HAVE A GREAT TIME; IT WAS FOR HERS AND
MINE.
NO ONE DOESN'T HAVE TO REALLY KNOW.
WE JUST GOT DOWN ON THE FLOOR.
WE MAY HAVE OUR DIFFERENCES -- ONLY HER AND ME.
THAT'S ME AND BEVERLY.
IF YOU HAPPEN TO SENSE LOVE,
 THEN YOU'LL KNOW WHAT THIS SONG IS ALL ABOUT.
WITH OR WITHOUT -- HEAR THIS SONG
 AND READ BETWEEN THE LINES;
YOU'LL KNOW WHAT IT'S ALL ABOUT.
WE DID DANCE ALL OVER THE FLOOR,
JUST HER AND I -- WE REALIZE WHAT IT WAS FOR.
I'M SURE YOU'VE FIGURED OUT THIS SONG.
WE JUST FEEL TOGETHER AND BELONG.
THAT'S ME AND BEVERLY.
HAPPY BIRTHDAY, BEVERLY

GOOD BYE, MY GYPSY LOVE

My Gypsy Love has never been confined.
She corrupted my spirit and my mind.
We never stood still, we tore up the town.
Yes, I've been lost, but now I stand my ground.

My Gypsy Love tried to lead me astray.
Like that black sheep, I was lost in my day.
I've worked hard for the love I once had.
Today, it's gone ---- for this I am glad.

My Gypsy Love was selfish and so unkind.
It took a long time to finally find,
Find a new love with a greater reward.
Today with faith I've found it in the good Lord.

My Gypsy Love chose the devil's way.
They may have my Gypsy and with them she can stay.
The Devil's people took a special part of me that day.
They made the fatal mistake when they took my daughter down Mexico way.
My Gypsy Love I'll fight her people to the end,
Don't care who I hurt or who I offend.
With the good Lord on my side, I go to Him and pray.
His answer was clear; Here's what he had to say....

Your misfortune was of the Devil's deed.
You've come to me with trust and a faithful smile.
I promised you I would answer your need.
I will give you your daughter after this trial.

You have been patient and believed in the love and word of mine.
For that, I'll give you another love that will be so special and divine.
This I know you're worthy of.
I'll fill your empty spot with your daughter's presence and love.

So, Good Bye, Gypsy Love, you were so unworthy and so unkind.

You've tormented my life. I'll forget it today.
I've found a new love; He promises me a peace of mind.
I'll obey the good Lord, His will and His way.

My Gypsy Love, I've turned my like around
I now praise the good Lord for His love that I have found.
My Gypsy Love was a costly mistake,
But it made me see what the good Lord can give and take.

Good Bye, Gypsy Love;
Thank you, O'Lord
For my new love.
Thank you, O'Lord
For my new love.

WARDEN ANNIE

I now have someone to look upon.
I do realize when the Lord stood me up
And gave me a testimonial song.
I've always wanted affection and happiness
Though bless me with her only if it's a must.
Take no false of my pride and wisdom
Bless her with my sincere givedom.
As with her I'll be blessed through our life
And continue with joy, love, and all of her and my happiness.

Let us be an example, just like a child living with a proper example.
That's my Warden Annie as she took me off the street.
I praise and care for her as she is wise and sweet.
If she ever shows you happiness and affection,
She'll put you in the right direction.
She'll now always be in my prayers
Because she, for everyone, does care.

Lord, bless Warden Annie!

MY HIGHER POWER

YESTERDAY IS GONE AND TOMORROW IS NEAR.
TODAY IS TODAY, JUST FOR A MOMENT I HESITATED TO
PRAY.
THIS IS MY REASON I CAN'T SING THIS SONG,
SO LET ME SHARE WITH YOU HOW I WENT WRONG.

I STARTED DRINKING, I DON'T EXACTLY KNOW WHEN,
BUT BECAUSE OF IT I'M IN THE PEN,
AND I CAN'T SEEM TO KEEP OR TRUST A FRIEND.
I'VE BEEN SO LONELY, BUT IN PUBLIC I'D SMILE AND
PRETEND.

FROM CITY TO CITY AND FROM STATE TO STATE
CHANGING MY IDENTIY TO KEEP MYSELF FREE UNTIL IT
WAS TOO LATE.
I WOKE UP WITH DOCTORS ALL AROUND,
WITH ELECTRODE PADDLES AND ALL STRAPPED DOWN.

SCREAMING AND YELLING INTO CONVULSIONS, I WAS IN
A KNOT.
KNOWING DEATH AFTER BEING REVIVED,
I WOKE UP IN A PADDED CELL WAY UP ON TOP.
I CONNED AND CONNIVED AS I PLEADED WITH THEM
ALL;
I THEN REALIZED IN A HYSTERIA I WAS OBSESSED WITH
DRUGS AND ALCOHOL.

I TRIED TO STAY CLEAN ON MY OWN;
I HAD TOO MUCH PRIDE TO ASK FOR HELP OR PICK UP THE
PHONE.
I DID SLOW DOWN TO A CRAWL;
WITHOUT SUCCESS I HAD TO HAVE ANOTHER SIP OF
ALCOHOL.

NOW, STILL ALIVE AND BACK IN PRISON;
YES, I RELAPSED AND IT WAS MY OWN DECISION.

I STARTED WITH FUN AND LAUGHTER AND TORMENTED
MYSELF INTO A PIT.
I JUST WASN'T WILLING TO QUIT.

I BECAME CLEAN ENOUGH TO REFLECT ON MY MISTAKES
OUT THERE.
IT'S OBVIOUS MY ONLY ANSWER IS PRAYER.
TODAY I'LL PRAY FOR MY SOBRIETY,
AND WITH THAT I TRUST I'LL MAKE IT IN OUR SOCIETY.

I NOW BELIEVE IN THE SERENITY PRAYER.
I RECITE IT DAILY KNOWING GOD, AS MY HIGHER POWER,

VISION OF MYSTERY

After leaving this place and returning again,
I knew I didn't any longer belong for I could sense the Devil lurking within.
Upon my arrival, I checked into a motel
And pulled the drapes back for the sun to come in.
I was saddened by how much this world is filling with sin.
Seems everybody's occupied with lust and greed,
Searching and seeking for things they don't really need.

Most of the people are lost.
You can see it in their face.
They're too busy . . .
I can't imagine them without any grace.

Curiosity, I took a walk around and checked out the peoples' faces.
They appeared to be always on the go but to the wrong places.
As I reached the street corner, I stopped and paused at the silent crowd.
Then, I praised Jesus for making me feel special and proud.
This place where I was first born is now a mystery.
Without the grace of God, no one's concerned about it's Seattle history.

The landscape may appear to be the Lord's land,
But I'd rather return to Sioux Falls where the people are spiritually grand.
I now pray daily for His guidance and direction.
I thank the Lord for the grace to choose and abide.
I allow Him to direct me for I can spiritually decide.

"THE DEVIL'S WEB"

I DO INVITE YOU INTO MY DEVILISTIC WEB.
I WILL CONFUSE YOU BEFORE ANTHING MAY BE SAID.
 FOLLOW ME AND LISTEN TO ME AS YOU CRAWL INTO MY WEB.
I WILL PROVE TO YOU SIN AND PROMISE YOUR FORSAKEN DEATH.
 CRAWL INTO MY WEB WITH A SLOW BREATH
 AND YOU WILL EXPERIENCE THE REST.
I WILL WRAP YOU TIGHT INTO MY WEB WHERE YOU WILL NOT GET LOOSE.
OUT IN REALITY YOU'LL BE HUNG WITHIN THEIR NOOSE.
SO, COME AND ENTER MY WEB;
YOU WILL NEVER KNOW YOU'RE DEAD.
THE SIN YOU HAVE DONE IS ALL OVER.
NOW IN MY WEB YOUR SIN IS NOW GONE FOR YOUR SIN WILL BE NO MORE RIDICULED OR SAID.
NOW WITHIN MY WEB THY DEVIL TOOK YOU AS HE EXPRESSED WHAT YOU DID.
 THOUGH YOU MAY BE RELEASED FROM YOUR SIN,
JUST REPENT AND I MAY LET YOU LIVE AGAIN.
ONLY A FORGIVEN FEW MAY LEAVE MY WEB.
THIS I SAY UNTO YOU AS YOU DECIDE.
I WILL WATCH YOU FOR WHAT YOU CHOOSE AND DECIDE.
IT WILL BE MY WAY, SO, WAKE UP AND PRAY.
WITH HONEST PRAYER AND DEVIL'S WEB WILL NEVER FORGET AND BE THERE.
 IF YOU CHOOSE YOUR OWN WAY,
THIS DEVIL WILL HAVE NO MORE TO SAY
AS YOU TURN YOUR WAY TO TO YOUR LORD AS YOU PRAY.
I WILL NOT BE ABLE TO CONTROL YOU AS YOU MADE YOUR CHOICE.
 I AM A FALLEN ANGEL AND LURE PEROPLE INTO MY WEB.
THOUGH IF THEY BELIEVE IN THY LORD,
THEY MAY GO ON THERE OWN RECORD.
MY WEB IS ALWAYS THERE SO YOU MUST BE PREPARED;
AND NOW YOU HEARD MY WARNING.

SO, YOU MUST NOT FRET OR WORRY.
 WITHOUT A DOUBT AND WITH ALL SINCERITY YOU MUST
BELIEVE WHAT IN MY WEB WHAT I AM TALKING ABOUT.
REMEMBER WHAT THIS STORY TOLD YOU ABOUT THE DEVIL'S WEB.
YOU ARE ALWAYS WELCOME AND YOU MAY LIVE OR YOU CAN CRAWL INTO MY WEB
 AS YOU WILL FOR SURE BE DEAD.
LIVE OR DIE.
NOW IS YOUR FINAL CHOICE FOR YOU CAN CONTINUE TO SIN OR YOU CAN REJOICE.
I WILL ALWAYS HAVE A PREPARED WEB;
SO TAKE HEED FOR WHAT I SAID.

THE DAY THAT I LEFT YOU

I REMEMBER THE DAY I LEFT YOU
AS I LEFT YOU ALL ALONE.
I TORE UP YOUR NUMBER
FOR I WOULDN'T BOTHER YOU ON THE PHONE.

OUR LOVE I KNOW WE RESPECTED,
BUT THE WAY I DID YOU JUST CAN'T BE JUSTIFIED OR
RESPECTED.
I NOW REALIZE IT'S OVER, AND WE MUST CONTINUE ON
WITH SOME OTHER.
JUST REMEMBER I LOVED YOU LIKE A WIFE, SISTER, AND
MOTHER.

YOU MEANT SO MUCH TO ME;
YOU DID WAKE ME UP AND THANK YOU, DARLING; YOU
CAUSED ME TO SEE.
I'LL NEVER FORGET YOU -- THAT DAY I LEFT YOU.
I'LL PROPOSE MYSELF BECAUSE YOU SHOWED ME WHAT I
MUST DO.
DARLING, FORGIVE ME AND MOST OF ALL I THANK YOU
FOR ALL WHAT YOU SHARED WITH ME.
DARLING, I'LL NEVER FORGET THE DAY I LEFT YOU;
WE MUST FORGET THE SAD TIMES AND START OVER LIFE
ANEW.

DANCING MY WHITE CADILLAC

Just out dancing in my white Cadillac
With my hydraulics and the batteries in the back.
Cruising up and down the street,
And I know the girls think it's sweet.
I come back to turn around and drop my caddy on the ground.
The girls stand and stare as I do beware.
Now I know where they all hang around,
Around my caddy as it lays on the ground.
They now call me Jumping Low
And they all know where I go.
I cruise the boulevard, cruise around
And then drop it in my yard.

They all want to dance;
I let it be known that I'm not ready for romance.
I crank the oldies loud and clear;
The home girls get up with it and stay near.
I pull out of the trunk a lot of beer and get close to one and hold her near.
Then, I whispered in her ear, "Home girl, you be with me and stay near."

Learned her name to be Crystal.
Then, holding her I found she held a pistol.
I found her super fine, but with her life style she'll never be mine.
So, now I'll go back out dancing my white Cadillac
And be careful who I meet when I get back.

It's all about dancing my white Cadillac.
Always cautious, I know I'll always dance back.
Because it was bought out of the showroom floor,
I'll be back with my first love as before.

I did not do no more drinking as I promised and worked hard.
I never stopped by no bar, but, Young Lady, you know how they and I
can be lead afar.
If I've done you wrong, I'll return this white Cadillac where it shall
belong.

HE WALKED 10 MILES

I KNOW YOU WALKED WITH US BEFORE;
WE SAVED YOU WHEN YOU KNOCKED UPON OUR DOOR.
WE ARE NATIVE AMERICANS, AND
THAT'S WHAT WE STAND FOR.

WE WILL UNITE WITH LOVE FOR ONE ANOTHER,
AS WE'LL STAND WITH PRIDE FOR EACH OTHER.
I FOUND THIS OLD WHITE MAN ALL WRINKLED UP ON
OUR ROSEBUD RESERVATION.
HE WALKED WITH HONOR, WITHOUT ANY HESITATION.

HE WAS HONEST AND TRUE.
AS HE WALKED 10 MILES WE KNEW HE'D MAKE IT
THROUGH.
HIS SHOES WERE TORN ALL ABOUT;
THEREFORE, WE HONORED HIM OUR MOCCASINS
WITHOUT A DOUBT.
HE WALKED THAT 10 MILES SHOWING US HIS RESPECT
WITH A GRACIOUS SMILE.
HE WILL ALWAYS BE WELCOMED ON OUR LAND FOR HE
SEEKS TO UNDERSTAND.

WE ALL KNOW HE'LL RETURN; FOR WE DO REALIZE WHAT
HE DID LEARN.
HE PROMISED TO RETURN WITH GIFTS AND FOOD AS WE'LL
WELCOME IN OUR SUN DANCE;
THERE HE AND OUR WARRIORS WILL DANCE, SHOUT, SING,
AND CHANTS.
THE OLD WRINKLED WHITE MAN WALKED THAT 10
MILES,
AND WITH PRIDE AND GRATITUDE WILL FOREVER KEEP
HIS PROMISE AND SMILE.

BACK BEHIND THESE
PRISON WALLS AGAIN

BACK BEHIND THESE PRISON WALLS AGAIN INSIDE THESE
WALLS WITHIN.
I'M WITH THE DEVIL, HIM AND I, HERE IN THIS CELL ALL
ALONE.
BECAUSE I'VE FAILED MY RECOVERY AND FAITH, I ALLOWED
THE DEVIL TO WIN.
I JUST HAD TO DRINK ONE MORE TIME; I DID IT ON MY
OWN.
I FEEL LIKE I HAVE DIED GOD KNOWS I'VE TRIED.

I LET THE DEVIL TAKE MY DAY; I LET HIM HAVE HIS WAY.
NOW, MY FAMILY AND I WILL PAY THE DEBTS.
BECAUSE I DRANK AGAIN THE OTHER DAY,
I MUST FACE MYSELF WITH ALL MY REGRETS.

I FEEL LIKE I COULD HIDE AND CRY
THAN BE BACK BEHIND THESE PRISON WALLS AGAIN.
BUT, TODAY I'D RATHER DIE
IF I'M DESTINED HERE TO LIVE IN SIN.

AS I LOOK IN THE MIRROR, I SEE NO TEAR
AND MY FRIENDS TELL ME I'LL NEVER MAKE IT OUT
THERE.
THOUGH I WALK PROUDLY DOWN THE CELL HALL, THEY
ALL CAN SENSE MY FEAR.
I LIE TO THEM AND TELL THEM I JUST DON'T CARE.
SO, I MAY DO LIFE BEHIND THIS PRISON WALL.
THIS IS WHERE I MAY REMAIN.
AT LEAST I WILL BE FREE FROM THE ALCOHOL
BACK BEHIND THESE PRISON WALLS AGAIN.

FOR THIS I SHALL PAY A SEVERE DEBT, SURELY YOU CAN
BET,
DWELLING IN THIS HOUSE OF SIN.

FOR THE REST OF MY LIFE HERE'S WHERE I'LL PROBABLY SIT,
BACK BEHIND THESE PRISON WALLS AGAIN.

THESE SOUTH DAKOTA WALLS

LORD, JUST HERE THE OTHER DAY IS THE FIRST TIME I
SEEN THESE WALLS.
I TRAVELED UP HERE FROM EL PASO TO SEE A DEAR FRIEND
OF MINE AND YOURS.
YES, LORD, I AM TALKING ABOUT THE PRISON HE'S IN HERE
IN SIOUX FALLS.
I ARRIVED THERE ABOUT THE TIME MY FRIEND WAS DONE
WITH HIS DAILY CHORES.

BUT, LORD, BEFORE I GOT THERE, I STOPPED BY THE RIVER
AND ADMIRED THE WATERFALLS;
AND, LORD, IT MADE ME THINK OF THE TEARS OF THOSE
PRISONERS INSIDE THE WALLS.
THE SUN WAS SETTING IN THE WEST; MY FRIEND AND I
SHOOK HANDS FOR THE FIRST TIME.
THOSE WALLS LOOKED CRUEL MADE OF RED GRANITE
AND LIME.

SO, LORD, WE BOTH KNOW WHY THOSE WALLS ARE
THERE,
AND WE KNOW WHY THE WATER RUNS OVER THE FALLS..
AND, LORD, WE KNOW WITH YOUR PROMISE AND LOVING
CARE
YOU WILL HELP THE PRISONERS BEHIND THOSE SOUTH
DAKOTA WALLS.

SOUTH DAKOTA WALLS --- SOUTH DAKOTA WALLS, HERE
YOU STAND.
HERE IS SIOUX FALLS YOU DIVIDE FREEDOM AND MANY
MEN IN THEIR CELL.
YES, LORD, THESE WALLS ARE THE AUTHORITY OF THIS
LAND.
YES, THE SOUTH DAKOTA WALLS HAVE MANY A STORIES TO
TELL ABOUT A LIVING HELL.

NOW, LORD, THIS HAS BEEN A JOURNEY FOR ME,
AND THIS HAS MADE ME TELL THE STORY OF THE SOUTH
DAKOTA WALLS.
I KNOW THAT THIS IS WHY I AM HERE AND WHAT YOU
WANTED ME TO SEE
AND UNDERSTAND, LORD, THE **SOUTH DAKOTA WALLS**
HERE IN SIOUX FALLS.

MY CONFIDANT

TO SUMMARIZE THIS STORY I WILL ADDRESS IT IN POETRY AND PROSE EXPRESSING MY SINCERE GRATITUDE AS I TELL YOU HOW THIS STORY GOES. THIS IS TO SHARE WITH YOU ABOUT MY WIFE, THE PERSON WHO HAD A LOT OF INFLUENCE IN CHANGING MY LIFE.

I INFATUATED HER WITH MY FRAUDULENT AND HUMOROUS LINES ,
AND WITH ILLUSIVE DECEIT I SHOWED HER SOME GOOD TIMES.
SHE KNEW I ABUSED DRUGS AND ALCOHOL AND OF MY BEHAVIOR SHE SOON LEARNED.
WITHOUT BEING NAÏVE AND FILLED WITH KINDNESS, SHE BECAME CONCERNED.

SHARING ALL MY HARDSHIPS, SHE WAS ASTOUNDED WITH HER TRAMATIC DISCOVERY AND STILL WAS WILLING TO HELP SEE ME THROUGH MY RECOVERY.
SHE HAS STOOD BY ME THROUGH SEVERAL INPATIENT TREATMENT CENTERS AND INSTITUTIONS
AND HAS SEEN ME THROUGH MANY DELIRIOUS TREMORS.

ALL THROUGH THESE STAGES OF MY ADDICTION SHE HAS BEEN VERY SUPPORTING.
THE PITY STOPPED; SHE ENABLED ME NO MORE.
THAT HAS BEEN REWARDING.
I AM VERY GRATEFUL TO HER AS SHE IS DILIGENT AND BEAUTIFUL, PROFICIENT,
AND THROUGH SOME TOUGH LOVE, IT'S PROVED TO BE SELF-EDUCATIONAL.

ABSTINENT FROM ALCOHOL AND APPRECIATING HER KINDNESS, I'M PROUD TO SAY AS WE HONOR OUR RELATIONSHIP,
"WE CHERISH OUR LOVE EVERYDAY."

TODAY SHE IS TRULY CONCERNED WHEN I APPEAR TO BE
DISCOURAGED;
SHE ALWAYS REMINDS ME OF HOW MUCH SHE LOVES ME
--
AND FOR THAT I'M ENCOURAGED.

WE NOW CAN COMMUNICATE REFLECTING THE PAST AND
HOW MISERABLE WE REALLY WERE.

BALLAD OF SOBRIETY

LAST NIGHT I PASSED OUT WITH AN UNHAPPY ENDING –
I WOKE UP TO A BAD START.
EVERY TIME I DRANK, BABE, SEEMS I TORMENTED YOUR
HEART.
I STARTED OUT LAST NIGHT LIKE ALWAYS BEFORE TO
FORGET
ABOUT MY PAST.
THAT FIRST DRINK I INTENDED FOR IT TO BE MY LAST.

I THOUGHT I'D RELAX AND HAVE JUST ONE
WHILE I THOUGHT ABOUT WHAT MY DRINKING HAS
DONE.
NOW I REALIZE I CAN'T DRINK NO MORE;
AND, WHEN I DO, YOU ALWAYS LOCK THE DOOR.
I COME IN LATE AT NIGHT AND TURN THE MUSIC ON;
I WAKE YOU UP AND THEN THE FIGHT WAS ON.
MY SPEECH IS SLURRED AND YOU GET ABSURD.
YOU DON'T HEAR A WORD I SAY; NO WONDER, BABE, YOU
FEEL THIS WAY.
WE ARGUE ANOTHER DAY.

I DON'T REMEMBER DRIVING HOME LAST NIGHT;
DON'T EVEN REMEMBER OUR FIGHT.
I DO REMEMBER YOU TELLING ME THAT I'M KILLING
MYSELF; AND IT IS TRUE,
I DO ADMIT I NEED SOME HELP, BUT WHAT DO I DO?

I KNOW I'M LOSING INTEREST, BABE, EVEN LOSING YOU.
I DON'T WANT TO DRINK NO MORE, WILL YOU HELP ME
PRAY?
PRAY FOR MY SOBRIETY AND FOR OUR LOVE THAT I JUST
DON'T DRINK TODAY.
BECAUSE I DON'T WANT TO LOSE YOUR LOVE
AND WILL ADMIT IT EVERY DAY.

I ONLY KNEW HER BY HER NAME

SHE LEFT A TEAR-STAINED NOTE UPON OUR DINING ROOM TABLE.
IT SAID TO CALL HER TONIGHT IF I WAS ABLE.
SHE'D BE DOWNTOWN AND ALL ALONE,
SO I CALLED ALL THE BARROOMS AND GOT HER ON THE PHONE.
I SAID, "YOU'RE NOT LEAVIN' ME WITH YOUR BLAME AND ALL ALONE."
THAT'S WHEN SHE SLAMMED DOWN THE TELEPHONE.

I ONLY KNEW HER BY HER NAME.
SHE LEFT ME STRANDED IN HER SHAME.
SHE TOOK IT ALL WITH HER BUT THE BLAME.
YES, I GUESS I ONLY KNEW HER BY HER NAME.

I CHANGED INTO MY WESTERN SUIT AND STETSON HAT AND LOADED UP MY .45.
I LUNGED INTO THE DARK BARROOM; THERE SHE WAS HANGIN' ON ANOTHER GUY.
MY HANDS WERE A-SHAKING AND MY O' HEART WAS A-ACHIN'.
I SQUEEZED THE TRIGGER OUT OF MY RAGE AND SHOUTED,
"YOU BOTH DESERVE TO DIE! AS SHE FELL TO THE FLOOR WITH A SILENT CRY."

SHE TOOK EVERYTHING BUT THE BLAME.
SHE LEFT ME STRANDED IN HER SHAME.
SHE TOOK EVERYTHING BUT THE BLAME.
I GUESS I ONLY KNEW HER BY HER NAME.

THE MAN THERE WITH HER CAME UP FROM THE BAR STOOL AND RAISED HIS HANDS.
HE FEARFULLY SAID, "MISTER, SHE WAS TELLIN' ME ABOUT ALL OF YOUR DEMANDS."

THERE WAS SILENCE IN THE ROOM AS MY GUN HIT THE FLOOR.
I WAS IN DOUBT AND DARKNESS -- AS I SENSED THE SILHOUETTE IN THE DOOR.
THAT'S WHEN I REALIZED I WENT TEMPORARILY INSANE.
I WAS CAUGHT UP IN A TRANCE -- NOW I'M DESTINED TO LIVE ALONE WITH HER
BLAME.
SHE TOOK EVERYTHING FROM ME BUT THE BLAME.
NOW I'M STRANDED AND LEFT IN HER SHAME.
SHE TOOK EVERYTHING FROM ME BUT THE BLAME.
YES, I GUESS I ONLY KNEW HER BY HER NAME

GREYHOUND BOUND

I PURCHASED MY TICKET FOR TO BE GREYHOUND BOUND,
TOLD THE TICKET MASTER I'M TIRED AND I JUST WANT TO
TRAVEL AROUND. NO MORE RAILS OR FLIGHT --
ALL I SEEK IS TO GET MY LIFE RIGHT.
TRAVELING FROM CITY TO CITY LOOKING OUT
THE WINDOW AND OBSERVING A LOT OF CARELESS PITY.
GETTING OFF IN VARIOUS WELL-KNOWN TOWNS,
I EXPERIENCED HAPPINESS AND A LOT OF FROWNS.
IT CAUSED ME TO MEDITATE ON WHAT AM I REALLY
LOOKING FOR.
THE BUS STOPPED AND I GOT OFF OUT OF THE DOOR.
I NOTICED A SMALL CHURCH ACROSS THE WAY.
BEING CURIOUS I WENT IN AND FELL TO MY KNEES
AND STARTED TO PRAY.
AFTER MY SINCERE PRAYER, THE GOOD LORD ANSWERED
AND SAID, " FOLLOW ME AS I FOR YOU WILL SHOW YOU
WHERE."
AS A LOST SHEEP IT WAS IN MY HEART I WAS THERE.
I'LL GIVE GREYHOUND BUS LINE SOME CREDIT
AND ADVISE OTHERS IT WILL BE FINE.
I WAS LOST BUT NOW I FINALLY FOUND MINE.
I THANK THE LORD AS HE FORGAVE ME OF MY SIN.
I'M BLESSED AND MY NEW LIFE HAS A CHANCE TO BEGIN.
MAY WE ALL BLESS THE LORD AND TRUST IN HIM;
HE WILL PROMISE TO DELIVER YOU FROM SIN.

AMEN

OUR WEDDING INVITATION

WE'RE DETERMINED TO HAVE A GLORIOUS CELEBRATION
INVITING ALL OUR FRIENDS AND OUR RELATIONS.
WE WILL CAUSE IT TO BE A SOBER WEDDING
WITH A NON-ALCOHOLIC SETTING.
WE'LL HAVE A GOOD TIME AND A LOT OF LAUGHTER
SHARING OUR FAITH FOR SERENITY IS ALL WE'RE AFTER.

AFTER WE'VE RECITED OUR WEDDING VOWS,
WE'LL THANK THE LORD FOR ALLOWING THIS TO BE
WITNESSED NOW.
WE'LL PRAISE HIM FOR TAKING AWAY OUR LONELINESS
AND DEPRESSION,
AND WITH EXPERIENCE, LEARNED AN IMPORTANT
LESSON.

OUR FRIENDS FROM OUR CHURCH PROMISE TO BE OF
INSPIRATION;
THEY'LL ALWAYS BE THERE WHEN WE'RE IN DOUBT OR IN
DESPERATION..
WITH THAT AND THE LOVE OF OUR SAINTS
WE'LL BE CONTENT FOR THEY'LL BE THERE FOR OUR
FUTURE COMPLAINTS.

SO, WITH ALL OUR FRIENDS HERE AND ABOUND
THROUGH GRACE WE'VE BEEN MARRIED ON MUTUAL
GROUND.

"WHAT AN INVITATION":
WITH THE GRACE OF GOD
THIS WILL BE A SERENE CELEBRATION.

REFLECTIONS

EACH NEW DAY GOD BRINGS OUR WAY
A FRESH OPPORTUNITY OF REFLECTION
AS WE PRAY FOR HIS DIRECTION.

RECEIVING HIM BRINGS INSTANT FORGIVENESS
AND ETERNAL GRACE;
DEATH IS A REAL PLACE.

DEATH IS CERTAIN BUT NOT THE END.
WE MUST REALIZE AND NOT PRETEND.

WE CANNOT ESCAPE STANDING BEFORE HIM;
WITHOUT HIM WE'LL LIVE IN SIN.
THERE IS NO EXCEPTION;
OUR ONLY HOPE IS IN JESUS CHRIST. . .
THROUGH HIS DEATH AND HIS RESURRECTION.

FAITH

I'VE FOUND IT HARD TO PRAY IN MY DIFFICULT SITUATIONS,
AND SOMETIMES DONE VERY LITTLE.
I USUALLY CHOSE THE EASY WAY OUT.
PLEADING IN MY MISCHIEVIOUS BEHAVIORS,
I'VE SEEN THE AFFLICTED AND DONE NOTHING TO HELP.
THESE PEOPLE HAVE BEEN THIS WAY PROBABLY
SINCE I DON'T KNOW WHEN AND LIVED IN
A WORLD OF SURVIVAL AND SIN.
WITH GOOD INTENTIONS, I ASK MYSELF WHAT IS MISSING
AND TODAY IT'S SIMPLE -
"FAITH".
I'VE FOUND MANY ANSWERS AND FOR ME TO FIND
ANSWERS
ASKED QUESTIONS. TO ASK QUESTIONS I'VE GAINED
KNOWLEDGE.
TO HAVE KNOWLEDGE I'VE BECAME WISER.
BEING WISER I CAN MAKE THE RIGHT DECISION
AND DECIDE WHAT I WANT IN LIFE.

A LETTER TO JESUS

JESUS,

I know You have saved me time after time as I've been praying for so long. Until I accepted You, I had no spiritual song. Now that I have one, I will be content with You where I now belong.

This is a short letter, Jesus, though in my heart I'll always have a special song. I want to be born again; trust me this time. I'm disgraced from crawling in sin. With my heart open and sincere, I trust You'll always walk with me and be near. Being a sinner as I am, I'll promise to do my best to follow Your commands and cleanse my mind to realize they are not just demands.

Jesus, take this letter, take this letter in heed. Take me in your hand and plant me as You would a seed. Give me a sign as I let You in. Oh, righteous Savior, deliver me from sin. When the time is here, I'll hear that trumpet blow, trusting You'll cleanse my body as pure as snow.

Jesus, I have no desire to be cast into Satan's lake of fire. Never again will I fret or doubt. Being born again is what faith is all about. Fear, hunger, or sorrow ----BELIEVING IN YOU, JESUS ---- I'll never have to worry about tomorrow.

Though this is a short letter, I want You to hear my prayers coming from my heart, mind, and soul. Upon the judgment day, I'll be on Your scroll. I will wait patiently for Your reply with trust and faith until the day this body will die.

HE CAME TO ME

I SILENTLY AWOKE AND RAISED MY HEAD;
SEEMS LIKE I WAS LIFTED LIKE NEVER BEFORE.
AS I FELT SOMETHING PULLING ME, I GOT OUT OF BED;
WITHOUT HARDLY KNOWING IT I HAD MY KNEES ON THE
FLOOR.

I THEN HEARD A VOICE NOTHING LIKE OUR OWN.
HE WHISPERED, "YOU OBEYED ME; TODAY I ALLOWED YOU
ANOTHER TRIAL."
A SILHOUETTE OF LIGHT SLOWLY PASSED LIKE I'VE NEVER
KNOWN.
MY EYES OPENED AND MY HANDS WERE HELD HIGH FOR
A LONG WHILE.

I FELT PRESSURE UPON MY SHOULDERS AS IT PENETRATED
WITHIN.
I WAS BLESSED WITH ENCOURAGEMENT; IT WAS ALL
OVER MY FACE. PRAYING OUT LOUD IN AN UNKNOWN
LANGUAGE, MY TONGUE BEGAN;
I TOOK A DEEP SERENE BREATH AND THANKED HIM FOR
HIS GRACE.

HE CAME TO ME FOR THE REST OF THAT NIGHT AND INTO
THE NEXT DAY. HE CAME TO ME; TODAY I WONDER WHAT
HE HAD ME SAY.

O'LORD, I'VE GOT YOUR NUMBER

O'LORD, I WANT TO REMIND YOU WHAT YOU ALREADY KNOW.
I HAVE FOUND SOME LOST SOULS OUT IN THE COLD.
SOME REMAIN IN PRISON AND OTHERS PLAYING OUT IN THE BARS.
THEYRE COMING BACK FOR DRUGS AND DRINKING AS THEY' RE
KILLING AND WRECKING CARS.

O'LORD, YOU SAID I MAY AT ANYTIME TO JUST CALL:
I'VE BEEN THERE AS WE GOT LOST;
SOME ARE WILLING TO PLAY NO MATTER WHAT THE COST.
THE POOR SOULS ARE EMPTY AS THEY PLAY THE DEVIL'S GAME;
SOME WILL ADMIT THAT THE DEVIL CAUSED THEIR GRIEF AND SHAME.

O'LORD, YOU ALLOWED ME TO WITNESS TO YOUR YOUNG AND TO ALL THE PRISONERS YOU WANTED IT TO BE SUNG/
PEOPLE OUT THERE, ESPECIALLY OUT IN THE COLD,
LET THEM NOT PARISH NEITHER YOUNG OR OLD.
I HAD TO CALL YOU TODAY.
I ASK IN MY PRAYERFUL CALL YOU'LL HEAR WHAT I HAVE TO SAY.
CLEANSE US ALL FROM THE DRUGS AND ALCOHOL.
O'LORD, I TRUST YOU ACCEPTED MY SINCERE CALL.
I TOLD THEM TO TAKE A GOOD LOOK AT ME HOW I TRY
JUST BELIEVE AND YOU MAY FALL A TEAR, BUT IT'S NOT A CRY.
REPENT TO THE LORD AND BE SINCERE,
FOR YOU'LL NEVER HAVE ANY FEAR.

THE PRECIOUS GIFTS

O'LORD, I'VE BEEN SILENT WITHOUT CHARITY OR TRUST.
ALWAYS DOUBTING YOUR WORD AND OCCUPYING MYSELF
IN LUST.
I NEEDED NO ONE -- TO REMAIN SILENT WAS A MUST.
O'LORD, I NEEDED NOBODY; OH, HOW YOU PROVED THAT
TO BE WRONG.
I NEVER KNEW REAL LOVE UNTIL I WAS QUOTED A
SPIRITUAL SONG.
IT WAS THEN I REALIZED WHAT I WAS MISSING ALL
ALONG.
WITH DOUBT, BUT SINCERE PRAYER, I WAS BAPTIZED IN
WATER;
(RECEIVING THE HOLY SPIRIT), IT WAS JUST THEN WITH
FAITH
MY NEW LIFE YOU PROMISED, NOW WOULD BEGIN.

O'LORD, I AM GRATEFUL YOU BLESSED ME WITH COURAGE
AND THE WISDOM TO UNDERSTAND
FOR IT IS YOUR GIFTS THAT WILL DIRECT ME AND WILL
GIVE ME A HELPING HAND.
O'LORD, YOU'VE GIVEN ME TWO PRECIOUS GIFTS:
                    THE HOLY SPIRIT IN MY SOUL AND
                    THE MIND TO PRAISE YOU WITHOUT
ANY DOUBT.
SINCE THAT DAY I'VE MADE A COMMITTMENT TO WITNESS
YOUR LOVE
 AND WHAT OTHER PEOPLE IN MY LIFE IS ALL ABOUT.

THE TRAIN TO JESUS

I HAD TO BOARD HIS TRAIN THAT WAS HEADING HIGH
AS I WAS STANDING STILL IN SHAME.
 I'VE NOTICED PEOPLE SMILING
AS THEY WAVED ON THEIR WAY BACK.
 I WONDERED WHAT MY STANDING STILL CAUSED ME TO
LACK. WITH DETERMINATION AND CURIOSITY IN MY
MIND,
 I BOARDED HIS TRAIN JUST TO SEE WHAT I COULD FIND.
 I DID REACH THE END OF THE LINE.
OH! MERCY! FOLLOW ME AS I FOUND EVERYTHING IS
FINE.
I THEN REALIZED HOW MISERABLY I WAS WRAPPED UP IN
SIN.
 I FELL TO MY KNEES AND FELT I COULD REPENT
 AND COULD NOW BEGIN.
 AS I RETURNED MY LIFE SEEMED TO BE OF SOLID FAITH.
 NOW THEN I BELIEVE IN HIS WORD AS HIS SPIRITUAL GRACE.
 THE OPPORTULNITY IS FOREVER THERE FOR US ALL.
 BOARD HIS TRAIN AND YOU TOO WILL HEAR HIS CALL.
 NOW, WITH MY SPIRITUAL LIFE I'M NOW
 BLESSED WITHOUT SIN AND STRIFE.
 I PRAY YOU ALL TO BOARD HIS TRAIN
 FOR YOU'LL NEVER LIVE IN SHAME.

HE IS COMING SOON IN A TWINKLE OF AN EYE

"I'M COMING SOON," HE SAYS, "LIKE A THIEF IN THE NIGHT."
IT WON'T BE MORNING OR NOON.
HE'LL COME IN A **TWINKLE OF AN EYE.**
THE BIBLE TELLS US WHY.
DON'T TAKE ME FOR A PROPHET.   THIS IS WHAT I'VE READ.
I'M ONLY TRANSCRIBING WHAT THE GOOD BOOK HAS SAID.
HE'LL BE HERE IN A **TWINKLE OF AN EYE.**
THIS HE PROMISES AND THE GOOD BOOK TELLS US WHY.
FOR WE'VE FELL SHORT OF THE GLORY OF GOD'S WAY
AND FOR ALL WHO SINNED, THEY, MUST PAY.
IT'S TIME TO REPENT ALL YE WOMEN AND MEN
FOR DEATH IS CERTAIN AS ARE THE WAGES OF YOUR SIN.
HE'LL COME IN A **TWINKLE OF AN EYE** FOR THE TIME IS NEAR.
REPENT, BE BAPTIZED IN HIS HOLY NAME.
YOU SHALL BE REBORN AND BE LIFTED WITHOUT ANY FEAR.
YOU SHOULD PUT YOUR MIND AT REST,
FOR WE'LL NEVER KNOW THE DAY OF HIS COMING OR FINAL TEST.   BEHOLD, FOR TODAY THE EAST AND WEST ARE FORSEEING THE ARMEGEDON WAR.
YOU'VE HEARD THE SCRIPTURE; AND WOE!
REPENT, FOR HE IS AT THE DOOR.
KNOCK, AND HE'LL LET YOU IN.
BE BAPTIZED AND HIS PROMISE WILL SAVE YOU FROM SIN.
EXCUSE NOT YOUR COLOR, RACE, OR CREED
FOR THOSE WHO CALL UPON HIM HE'LL REJUVINATE YOUR SOUL AS A NEW-BORN SEED. HE'LL COME IN A **TWINKLE OF AN EYE** AS THE GOOD BOOK SAID. BELIEVE NOT AGAINST HIS WORD. FOR, IT IS ALL TRUE --

ALL THAT I'VE READ. HE'LL BE HERE SOON AS A **TWINKLE IN AN EYE** AT ANY DAY. IT IS ONLY FOR HIM TO KNOW. SO, WE MUST PREPARE FOR HIS WAY.
HE'S COMING SOON IN A **TWINKLE OF AN EYE**.
SO, READ YOUR BIBLE AND UNDERSTAND IT WELL
TO GAIN KNOWLEDGE AND WISDOM.
IT WILL FREE YOU FROM YOUR BURDENS
AND FROM THE BRIMSTONES OF HELL.

AWAKE, CHRISTIAN SOLDIERS

WE MUST RALLY TO HIS CALL; THE ARMAGEDON IS NEAR, SO WE WILL NOW STAND ONCE AND FOR ALL.

HIS FALLEN ANGEL TORMENTED US ALL TOO LONG. THE LORD PROMISED THAT WHO SO BELIEVETH IN HIM WE WILL ARISE AND WITH HIM WE WILL BELONG.

SO, AWAKE, CHRISTIAN SOLDIERS, THE END OF TIME IS NEAR. AWAKE WITH PRAYER AND YOU'LL HAVE NO REASON TO FEAR.

I NEVER KNEW JESUS

I NEVER KNEW JESUS TIL I WAS FILLED WITH THE HOLY
GHOST.
NOW, I AM GRATEFUL FOR HIS LIFE HE GAVE FOR ME ON
THE CROSSED POST.
I WAS BAPTIZED IN THE WATER AND RECEIVED HIS SPIRIT
AFTER STUDYING THE BOOK OF ACTS; HIS WORD I WILL
ALWAYS PROCURE IT.

COMING UP FROM THE WATER I CONFESSED FROM MY
SOUL
AND HEARD THE WORDS VIBRATE FROM MY LUNG.
MY SINS AND GUILT VANISHED AS I SPOKE TO THE LORD
WITH A FOREIGN TONGUE.
THIS I KNOW WAS NOT FOR ME TO KNOW OR
UNDERSTAND
THOUGH READING THE GOOD BOOK, I BELIEVE HIS WORD
AND HIS PLAN.
IT EASED MY DOUBTS AND MY MIND TO KNOW I HAVE
COMMUNICATED WITH HIM.
EVER SINCE THAT MOMENT I HAD ALL THE PROOF THAT
HE FORGAVE ME OF MY SIN.

THOSE TEMPORARY ACTS OF SIN ARE NOT WORTH
JEOPARDIZING HIS PROMISE AND REWARD.
THEREFORE, I MUST BE OBEDIENT; I MADE A COMMITMENT
TO JESUS, OUR LORD.
IT WON'T BE EASY TO TURN FROM SATAN'S TEMPTATIONS
IN THIS DAY AND AGE
AND I MUST CONSIDER HIS PROMISE OF THE FAMINE,
PLAGUE, WARS, AND RAGE.

THANK YOU, O', LORD, FOR THE DAY OF THE PENTECOST.
I TRUST YOU'LL DELIVER ME FROM THE 3-SCORE 666
NUMBER AND THEIR HOLOCAUST.
MY SINCERE PRAYER GOES OUT TO THOSE WHO ARE NOW
LOST.

O', LORD, GUIDE ME IN YOUR WAYS; I'LL SACRIFICE NO
MATTER WHAT THE COST.
BLESSED ARE THOSE WHO READ AND HEAR YOUR WORD
OF PROPHECY FOR THE TIME IS COMING NEAR.
BLESSED THOSE WHO TAKE YOUR LOVE TO HEART AND
PRAISE YOUR NAME FROM FEAR.

OUR LORD BROUGHT ME ABOUND

OUR LORD PUT ME ON SOLID GROUND,
GAVE ME THE STRENGTH TO CARRY ON.
NOW WITH FAITH AND WISDOM HE ALLOWED ME TO SEE
WHAT I AM ABOUT TO BE.
I NEED TO PRAY EVERY DAY.
BLESS OUR LORD AS HE GIVES US THE WORDS WHAT TO
SAY.
THAT'S WHY WE MUST OBEY.
YES, THE GOOD LORD BROUGHT ME ABOUND
AS NOW HIS WORDS WILL CARRY ON.
WITH TRUST AND FAITH BELIEVETH IN HIM
AND YOU'LL NEVER MAKE ANY MISTAKE.
MAY WE EXPRESS HIS PROMISED WORD AROUND.
BELIEVE IN HIM AND YOU'LL WALK ON SOLID GROUND.
WALK WITH TRUST AND FAITH WITH LOVE --
WITHOUT DISGRACE.

INSPIRING DREAMS

IN THE NAME OF JESUS –
YOU'RE IN MY DREAMS NIGHTLY;
WITHOUT YOU I'D TAKE LOVE LIGHTLY.
IN THE NAME OF JESUS –
ALLOW ME TO APOLOGIZE POLITELY.
THANK YOU FOR NOT GIVING UP ON ME.
YOU KNOW I'M SINCERELY TRYING.
YOU GAVE MY SOUL THAT WHICH STIRS MY HEART FROM CRYING.
BEFORE I ACCEPTED YOU, LORD, YOU HAVE LET ME GO ASTRAY.
NOW THAT I TRUST IN YOU, I KNOW IN MY HEART YOU'LL BE WITH ME TO STAY FOREVER EACH AND EVERY DAY.
I'VE CAUSED MANY SORROWFUL TEARS;
NOW, WITH STRENGTH AND FAITH YOU'LL BECOME A REALITY OF MY DREAMS THE REST OF MY YEARS.
SHOULD MY PILLOW BE SOAKEN WET WHEN I AWAKE –
I'LL REMEMBER MY DREAM EACH NIGHT WITH ANOTHER DAY BLESSING ME WITH WISDOM, FAITH, AND SIGHT.

THE RISEN LORD

THEY CRUCIFIED THE SON OF GOD NEARBY A HILLSIDE CAVE.
THEN TOOK HIS BODY FROM THE CROSS AND LAID IT IN THE GRAVE. THEY SET A ROMAN GUARD TO WATCH AND CLOSED AND SEALED THE TOMB. THE TRAITORS ALL WERE SATISFIED FOR THEY HAD SEALED HIS DOOM. THREE DAYS AND NIGHTS SEALED IN THE CAVE AND THEN OUR LORD AROSE. THE VICTORY OVER DEATH AND HELL AND OVER ALL HIS FOES.
IT WAS FOR ME HE LIVES, AND BY GOD'S GRACE TO SINFUL MAN'S ETERNAL LIFE, HE GIVES. AN ANGEL FROM THE GLORY CAME AND ROLLED THE STONE AWAY
FOR ALL TO SEE THAT HE AROSE ON THAT FIRST EASTER DAY.
THANK GOD IN HIM I NOW REJOICE REDEEMED BY HIS GRACE WHO DIED, YET LIVES TODAY AND INTERCEDES AT GOD THE FATHER'S SIDE.
"HE IS NOT," THE ANGEL SAID.
COME SEE THE EMPTY PLACE AND SEEK HIM NOT AMONG THE DEAD.
BUT, THANK GOD FOR HIS GRACE.
THEN YIELD UNTO THE RISEN LORD TO GUARD AND GUIDE THE WAY.
FOR HE WHO DIED AND ROSE AGAIN WILL LEAD HIS OWN TODAY.
FOR HE ALLOWS US A TESTIMONIAL AND GIVES US THE GRACE TO PRAY.

THE LORD'S SEED

"LORD, I AM YOUR SEED," THEREFORE I DO NOT WANT TO BE FALLEN UPON THE ROCKS, WHERE I CANNOT GROW AND FLORISH.

NO, NOT CASTED IN THE THORNS THAT WILL PARTIALLY TAKE ROOT, BUT BE AMONG THE SEEDS THAT FALL ON YOUR RIGHTEOUS SOIL AND BRING FORTH GOOD FRUIT, NO, I WON'T GROW WITHOUT YOUR GRACE OR SPIRIT.

IT IS EVIDENT THAT YOU HAVE A REASON FOR ME HERE; YOU PROMISE ME SUNSHINE - TO GROW "SPIRITUALLY." RAIN - TO GROW "HEALTHY." WARM SEASONS - TO "TRAVEL WITH YOUR WORD". COLD SEASONS - TO STAY STILL, TO "OBSERVE." YOU PROMISE ME WIND - TO "DISTRIBUTE AND MULTIPLY."

SOON THE TIME MUST COME WHEN I AM TO FLORISH AND ABIDE; FOR YOU GAVE ME A MIND TO "CHOOSE AND DECIDE."

AS A SEED GROWING IN RIGHTEOUS SOIL, I WILL DECAY, THE SPIRIT IN ME SHALL THEN RAISE. THEN I'LLUNDERSTAND THAT THIS LIFE HERE WAS A TEMPORARY TRIAL AND PHASE.

"THANK YOU, LORD, FOR GIVING ME A SOUL TO GIVE YOU PRAISE."

JESUS
GAVE HIS LIFE FOR MANY

Why did he need to do that?

What must you do to
benefit from it?

"REPENT"

— I SAITH UNTO YOU —

DANCING MY WHITE CADILLAC

Just out dancing in my white Cadillac
With my hydraulics and the batteries in the back.
Cruising up and down the street,
And I know the girls think it's sweet.
I come back to turn around and drop my caddy on the ground.
The girls stand and stare as I do beware.
Now I know where they all hang around,
Around my caddy as it lays on the ground.
They now call me Jumping Low
And they all know where I go.
I cruise the boulevard, cruise around
And then drop it in my yard.

They all want to dance;
I let it be known that I'm not ready for romance.
I crank the oldies loud and clear;
The home girls get up with it and stay near.
I pull out of the trunk a lot of beer and get close to one and hold her near.
Then, I whispered in her ear, "Home girl, you be with me and stay near."

Learned her name to be Crystal.
Then, holding her I found she held a pistol.
I found her super fine, but with her life style she'll never be mine.
So, now I'll go back out dancing my white Cadillac
And be careful who I meet when I get back.

It's all about dancing my white Cadillac.
Always cautious, I know I'll always dance back.
Because it was bought out of the showroom floor,
I'll be back with my first love as before.

I did not do no more drinking as I promised and worked hard.
I never stopped by no bar, but, Young Lady, you know how they and I can be lead afar.

If I've done you wrong, I'll return this white Cadillac where it shall belong.
HELP ME SWEET JESUS

WHITE CADILLAC

HONEY, HEY HONEY, WON'T YOU BUY ME THAT WHITE
CADILLAC,
THE ONE IN THE WINDOW SITTING IN THE BACK?
LET'S JUST TAKE IT FOR A RIDE;
THEN, YOU CAN DECIDE.
I PROMISE I'LL WORK EVERY DAY AND BRING YOU HOME
ALL MY PAY. WON'T BE STOPPING AFTER FOR A DRINK,
I'LL COME RIGHT HOME AND HELP YOU WITH THE CHORES
AND THE DISHES IN THE SINK. REMEMBER HOW I USED TO
OPEN YOUR DOOR?
I'LL DO IT AGAIN JUST LIKE BEFORE.
YOU'LL NEVER SEE IT AT A BAR;
IT'LL BE OUR FAMILY CAR.
DON'T WORRY ABOUT IT GETTING IMPOUNDED AT ALL;
I'M NOT DRINKING NO MORE ALCOHOL.
WE CAN CRUISE IN THE COUNTRY FOR A SPECIAL CRUISE
OR OUT TO THE LAKE FOR A SNOOZE.
DRIVE TO THE MOUNTAIN WHERE WE USED TO PARK
AND LISTEN TO OUR OLD MUSIC IN THE DARK.
WE'LL GAZE OFF INTO THE CITY LIGHTS AND REMINISCE
IN THE NIGHT. ILL KEEP MY WORD AND NEVER TAKE IT
BACK,
HONEY, IF ONLY YOU'LL BUY ME THAT WHITE CADILLAC.

I'LL KEEP MY PROMISE NEXT TIME

WHEN WE WERE YOUNG AND LONELY, I PROMISED YOU EVERYTHING.
I WHISPERED THAT I LOVED YOU AND YOU SLIPPED ON MY RING.
I PROMISED YOU MY LOVE, DEAR, BUT CAUSED YOU SO MUCH PAIN.
TO HURT YOU WITH A BROKEN PROMISE, I MUST BE INSANE.

WHEN WE WERE YOUNG AND LONELY, I PROMISED YOU MY LOVE. DARLING, WON'T YOU FORGIVE ME?
I'LL MAKE IT UP NEXT TIME.
DARLING, WON'T YOU FORGIVE ME?
YOU MAY KEEP MY RING.
KEEP IT ON YOUR FINGER; I'VE RUINED EVERYTHING.

WON'T YOU FORGIVE ME THIS BROKEN PROMISE OF MINE?
I'LL KEEP YOU IN MY MEMORY AND KEEP MY PROMISE THIS TIME.

WHEN WE WERE YOUNG AND LONELY, I PROMISED YOU MY LOVE. DARLING, WON'T YOU FORGIVE ME?
I'LL KEEP MY PROMISE NEXT TIME.
DARLING, WON'T YOU FORGIVE ME?
I'LL KEEP MY PROMISE NEXT TIME.

A WRITTEN PROMISE

AS I WENT TO SLEEP LAST NIGHT, I FELT SOMETHING WAS
WRONG,
AND I WOKE UP THIS MORNING WITH A SONG.
I THANKED THE LORD FOR MY DAILY DIRECTION.
HIS REPLY WAS WITH CHARITY AND AFFECTION.
I REACHED OVER FOR MY PAPER AND PEN
WHEN IT ALL CAME TO ME JUST THEN.

TODAY WAS ON THE SABBATH DAY; HE TOLD ME TO REST
AND WRITE.
I THEN RESTED AS I PRAYED, AND IT WAS THEN I SAW HIS
LIGHT.
HE GAVE ME A VISION OF MY LIFE BEING REBORN.
I AM TO FOLLOW HIM THE REST OF HIS WAY, AND MY SOUL
WILL NEVER BE TORN.
HE TOLD ME TO WRITE HIS PROMISE AND SPREAD IT
AROUND.
HE PROMISES US SALVATION AND A BETTER LIFE ON HIS
RIGHTEOUS GROUND.

SO, BEFORE YOU GO TO SLEEP, THANK HIM IN PRAYER AND
BELIEVE WITH FAITH
FOR HIS PROMISE AND HIS GRACE.
AFTER YOU'VE HAD A NIGHT OF REST AND THEN AWAKE,
YOUR DAY IS PROMISED FOR THE LORD'S SAKE.

A LETTER FROM JESUS

I love you; I shed my own blood for you to make you clean. You are new, so believe what I say is true. You are lovely in my eyes, and I created you to be just as you are. Do not criticize yourself or get down for not being perfect within yourself. This will only lead to frustration. I ask you to trust me and take one day at a time. Live and let God. Dwell in my power and love and you shall be free. Be yourself. Don't allow other people to discourage you. Beware of my presence in everything you do. I give you patience, direction, truth, and peace. Look to your saints for your answers. They'll act as your shepherds as you seek prayer. Follow my ways. Do not forget this. Listen and be patient for I will show you my will.

I love you. Let me be with you in everything that you do. Be not so concerned with yourself, as you are my responsibility. I will change you without you hardly knowing it. You are to also love yourself and to love others simply because I love you. Take your eyes off yourself and look at me. I lead; I change; I make. Your life has no time for selfishness.

I won't fight your efforts. Let me have the joy of making you like Christ. Let me give you joy, peace, and kindness. No one else can. You have proved that to yourself. You belong to me through my blood, never to yourself and never to others.

Don't complicate life. Relax in your faith and my love for you. My will is perfect. My love is sufficient. Look to me. I'll love you if you'll allow me to. I am personally involved with your life especially when you are suffering. I permit weakness and trials so you may come to me to depend totally upon my strength. Trials provide opportunities to know me better. Knowing me is the secret to a full and blessed life, as I choose it for you only.

AMEN

ECHOES OF ALCOHOLISM

I CRAVED ITS EFFECTS FROM MY CRIB TO CHILDHOOD;
RIDICULED AND WAS WARNED THAT IT IS NO GOOD.
ONCE ADDICTED WITH THE DESIRE TO STOP -- ONLY IF I
COULD.

RATHER GENETIC, HEREDITARY, OR MERELY A DISEASE,
SOCIALLY ACCEPTED AND DEFINITELY SOUGHT TO
PLEASE.

OBVIOUSLY IN MY ACTIONS AND EVERYTHING SAID,
CONTINUALLY OBSESSING ME DAILY AND LONG INTO
BED.

THE ECHOES OF ALCOHOLISM THAT I ABUSED FAR INTO
MY TEENS
DISRUPTED RELATIONS AND MY EDUCATION THAT
SHATTERED MY DREAMS.

PROVED FALSE COURAGE TO MANIPULATE MY SCHEMES
AS IT PROVOKED ME WITH DEVIOUS FRAUDULENT
SCHEMES.
THE ALCOHOL COMFORTABLY BECAME A WAY OF MEANS.

THE ALCOHOL IRRATICALLY IN MY TWENTIES EMOTIONALLY
ENGRAVED,
MY DESIRE OF IT I SEEKED AND CRAVED.

DRANK DAILY JUST FOR TEMPORARY RELIEF;
MY VALUES AND THOUGHTS WERE CORRUPTED WITH
GRIEF.
UNABLE TO COPE IN SOCIETY WITH MISERY AND SHAME,
I THEN REALIZED BECAUSE IT WAS TO BLAME.

NOW ABSTINENT FROM IT I NOW WITH CONFIDENCE WILL
NO LONGER LIVE IN DISTORTED SHAME.

FACES

FACES ARE NOT PAINLESS, I WON'T DENY.
THEY WILL ALWAYS BE WITH US AND CANNOTLIE.
SOMETIMES WITH HAPPINESS, SOMETIMES WITH SORROW,
OTHERS WITH DOUBT, IF THERE WILL BE ANOTHER TOMORROW.
THEY CAN BE EASILY REARRANGED; I WILL AGREE.
LOOK DEEP INTO A MIRROR, YOU'LL ALSO SEE
FACES CHANGE DAILY, I KNOW.
WE ALL HAVE EXPRESSIONS; YOU CAN SEE IT IN OUR FACIAL
GLOW.
A FACE MAY APPEAR TO EXPRESS WE'VE DONE WRONG.
FRET NOR WORRY … WE CAN CHANGE IT … IT DON'T HAVE
TO BE THAT WAY;
AND, IT DON'T HAVE TO LAST ALL DAY LONG.

EPILOGUE

... TO CONCLUDE THIS BOOK OF POETRY AND PROSE, I HAVE CONDENSED THESE POEMS TO BE INFORMATIVE FROM A CHAPTER OF REAL-LIFE EXPERIENCES OR SITUATIONS.

TO READ A MULTI-PAGE BOOK OF AN UNPUBLISHED AUTHOR, TO MOST, WOULD BE INSIGNIFICANT. YOU MAY AGREE AFTER CONTEMPLATING THESE CONTENTS. WITHOUT FINDING MY SPIRITUALITY AND THE WILLINGNESS TO CHANGE, I WOULD EASILY BE A WELL-KNOWN PUBLISHED AUTHOR ON A MOST-WANTED POSTER. YOU WILL AGREE **THAT** LIFE WOULD BE PURE HELL AND MISERY. MY PURPOSE OF SHARING THIS BOOK IS TO HOPEFULLY GIVE SOME POSITIVE ADVICE AND INSIGHT FOR THOSE WHO HAVE EXPERIENCED SIMILAR SITUATIONS OR SOMEONE FOR ENCOURAGEMENT, AS I AM DIRECTING THIS IN A CARING MANNER. IF IT WAS MEANT TO BE OF ALL SADNESS, THEN IT WOULDN'T BE OF ANY PURPOSE TO BE INFORMATIVE, MOREOVER, INTERESTING. THEREFORE, I WOULD ENCOURAGE YOU TO SERIOUSLY READ THIS BOOK.

I CHOSE THE TITLE, "ADDICTED AND CONVICTED" FOR MOST ARE ADDICTED TO SOMETHING OR ANOTHER. (OR POSSESSED). PRO OR CON. POSITIVE OR NEGATIVE. MOST ARE CONVICTED RATHER TO A BEHAVIOR, INCARCERATION, POSSESSION, OR SPIRITUALITY.

TODAY I CHOSE TO BE ADDICTED TO LIFE -- "I WANT TO LIVE."
TODAY I CHOSE TO BE CONVICTED SPIRITUALLY -- "I WANT PEACE."
TODAY I HAVE A HUMOROUS SAYING: "I COULD BARELY SEE OUT OF MY LEFT EAR AND COULDN'T HEAR OUT OF MY RIGHT EYE." TODAY, THOUGH, I AM NOW OK.

TO THINK NEGATIVE IS TO FAIL. TO THINK POSITIVE IS TO BE POSITIVE AND PROGRESSIVE. I HOPE THIS BOOK WILL ENCOURAGE YOU AS YOU SHARE IT WITH ANOTHER. IT TOOK ME FORTY YEARS TO REALIZE IT. SO, READ ON AND ENJOY! GOD BLESS.